WHAT BLACK MEN SHOULD DO NOW

D1403323

WHAT BLACK MEN SHOULD DO NOW

■ ■ ■ ■ ■

100 Simple Truths, Ideas, and Concepts

K. Thomas Oglesby

With a Foreword by Tavis Smiley

Kensington Publishing Corp.
http://www.kensingtonbooks.com

DAFINA BOOKS are published by

Kensington Publishing Corp.
850 Third Avenue
New York, NY 10022

Copyright © 2000, 2002 by K. Thomas Oglesby

All Kensington titles, imprints, and distributed lines are available at special quantity discounts for bulk purchases for sales promotions, premiums, fund raising, educational, or institutional use. Special book excerpts or customized printings can also be created to fit specific needs. For details, write or phone the office of the Kensington special sales manager: Kensington Publishing Corp., 850 Third Avenue, New York, NY 10022, attn: Special Sales Department, phone 1-800-221-2647.

Dafina Books and the Dafina logo Reg. U.S. Pat. & TM Office

ISBN 0-7582-0171-0

First hardcover printing: October 2000
First trade paperback printing: May 2002

10 9 8 7 6 5 4 3 2 1

Printed in the United States of America

This one is for you, my brothers. May it speak to you personally and help you strike balance in your lives.

CONTENTS

FOREWORD

A few years ago someone got the not-so-brilliant idea to start referring to black men as an "endangered species." I suspect the use of this term was an attempt to characterize a group of men who, I believe, is one of the most maligned in American history.

I hate the term *endangered species*. It makes me feel like a spotted owl or a bald eagle. I prefer to think of myself not as hunted prey on the verge of being extinct, but rather as a proud black man. Not unlike most black men I know, I have a capable, giving, willing, and positive presence. We can say it loud: "I'm a black man, and I'm proud!"

The truth is, while black men may not be an "endangered species," we *do* have issues, some of which we are not even aware that we have. Like other men, there are areas where black men fall short—from comfortably expressing our deepest emotions and volunteering in our communities, to maintaining proper health and enjoying rich relationships with our mates. It is critical that we address our challenges in this new millennium. We should seize this moment as an opportunity for black men to rediscover, redevelop, and define our purpose on this planet. More and more, I get the sense that too many black men don't accept the proposition that we do have a purpose on this planet. Purpose can be defined as a principle around which we organize our lives. In essence, our purpose is to be the best fathers, brothers, husbands, friends, and lovers. We must be creative, caring, competent, and productive men. Not rocks, not trees, not brick nor mortar but men—bold, beautiful black men.

We must be about the business of continually shaping our purpose. Each day of our lives we journey a little farther down the pathway of purpose, we move closer to a meaningful understanding of who we are. In doing so we can come to know peace, find time to play, and grow more in tune with our inner spirit. Shaping our purpose is a challenge we must be prepared to face.

It is very clear to me that my generation is the first generation of African Americans since the civil-rights struggle to advance to positions of leadership, responsibility, and authority. Men of my era were born at the tail end or just after the movement. Courageous black men before us paved the way for the progress we enjoy today. Their blood, sweat, and tears—indeed their lives—cannot be taken for granted. It's unclear just what Black America will look like a few years down the road with us leading the way, without a firsthand perspective on what the struggle was all about.

However, as black men, our charge is to continue the legacy of courage, boldness, and truth. In this new millennium, we need black men who will fight the good fight, keep the faith, and finish the course. We must be committed to knowing our history and ourselves. Then and only then can we begin not only to resolve our issues, but to shape our purpose.

When Ken and I met, he shared with me his vision for what you will read between the covers of this book. I was impressed by his positive energy and unlimited ability for clear and open expression. As African-American men, we agreed the topics were timely and the need was great. I jumped at the chance to write the foreword to this book for one simple reason: *This* book is a practical and useful guide to help black men—indeed all men—shape their purpose. It is full of life-changing strategies that can be applied daily.

The wise man Solomon once said, "With all thy getting, get understanding." As we seek to be understood, we must also seek to understand self, sister, and society. It is refreshing to see a book offering black men a dose of encouragement, hope, and enlightenment. I believe Ken has made a contribution to this effort through the writing of *What Black Men Should Do Now*. I trust you will agree.

Keep the faith.

Tavis Smiley
May 2002

PREFACE

*It takes a deep commitment to change and an even
deeper commitment to grow.*

—Ralph Ellison

During the historic 1995 Million Man March, 1.2 million African-American men from all walks of life assembled in the
nation's capital. It was a day black men joined hands, prayed
for peace, and pledged self-responsibility. It was a day when
we sang, rejoiced, and celebrated. We shared. We laughed.
We cried. And we did it all together as the world watched.
The march served as an impetus that ignited a new movement among brothers toward creating better lives for themselves, their families, and their communities. Today, in the
new millennium, black men in America must continue to
move onward in their quest to live healthier, more empowered, and spirited lives. We must do the necessary follow-up
by honoring those pledges—each and every one of us. And
based on the current plight of black men in this country, our
survival depends on it.

One would think that awareness and acknowledgment of
the critical state in which African-American men live would
prompt their immediate action to turn the tide. However, it is
not that simple. The age-old "script of manhood" that society
has handed men, particularly black men, is one that is nearly
impossible for them to follow and still maintain some sense
of humanness, not to mention their sanity. The script's meaning for the individual man is shaped less by biology than by a
cultural script or story. And that script is made up of societal

codes that guide, and at times pressure him into certain ways of acting and of understanding himself as a man. Moreover, this unrealistic script dictates that we must always conquer and control, be men of steel who don't get sick, and incessantly downplay our vulnerabilities. In general, men simply don't do vulnerability well; we view it as a flaw in our masculinity. It's not that we don't know vulnerability when we feel it—we do; however, men in this country are groomed to handle their physical and emotional issues differently than women, who, on the whole, are more attuned to self-care and nurturing. Maybe they are from Venus and we are from Mars, but black men have simply got to overcome these "barriers" that prevent us from living whole lives, rather than the half, fragmented ones we are virtually told we are supposed to live.

Generations of men have remained detached from their emotions, their mates' needs, each other in the name of brotherhood. Still today, we are laggard to respond when it comes to our own self-care and -nurturing, for fear of our manhood being challenged. Thus, many brothers live unconsciously and remain lost on the path of self-destruction. Sadly, the inherited manhood script in our society has placed an extremely heavy burden upon black men. Yet we continue to play it out, no matter how high the physical and psychological stakes. Well, guess what—it's a new day, and it's time we shed our archaic ideas of what it is to be an authentic man!

This book is not meant to strip you of your masculinity, transform you into some spineless pansy, whipped partner in your relationship, or milquetoast creature. Certainly *none* of us want (or need) to be that. We enjoy and celebrate manhood and appreciate the way we were "wired" by the Creator! Nor is this book meant to wag a scolding finger at black men for "bad behavior." This book's purpose, rather, is to entice you to bask in the abundance of living as a *whole* man by striking balance in your life. When you do, you'll wonder how you lived the way you did before.

As we navigate our way though this age of homicide, corporate-downsizing, cell phones, AIDS, Palms, and the Internet, some of us soar to the sky, while others fall by the wayside. May the brothers who maneuver with ease stay on the path, all the while giving a hand up to the men who are clueless wanderers in need of direction. We can draw strength from each other, and the sisters who love us, to begin to heal.

In the spirit of the Million Man March, *What Black Men Should Do Now: 100 Simple Truths, Ideas, and Concepts* was written to offer inspiration, encouragement, and reinforcement to African-American men—we who have been labeled an "endangered species." While our plight does look bleak, there is hope. But that hope can only be realized when we understand what we need to do to take control of our lives emotionally, physically, and spiritually.

Abundance and joy is our birthright, brothers. Our personal well-being has already been paid for—our ancestors secured it through their blood, sweat, and tears. But as is the case for any man—black, white, Technicolor—you must be willing to do a few things to redeem the reward. And it takes only a strong, personal desire to incorporate a few common-sensical changes into the way you live in this world.

This book represents a compilation of basic tools you can use to begin to effect change in your life. The one hundred simple truths, ideas, and concepts, which I call "strategies," can guide you on the journey to experiencing life in a more fulfilling way. Many of the strategies are pieces of advice collected from brothers (and sisters) around the country. Some of the strategies are based on personal experience and knowledge I have gained. The bulk of it, however, comes straight from common sense. You'll find some of the ideas obvious and some of the concepts radical. Some of the simple truths that reveal the things men do, don't do, feel and say, you will find to be laugh-out-loud funny. So, go on and laugh, brother—it's healthy and good for the soul!

While reading, you may discover that you relate well to certain ideas presented here. There may be others to which you feel no connection. Whether or not you get with them may hinge on your personal philosophies, ideas, or religious beliefs. Help yourself to what you want and need, because this book offers a lot to digest. For this reason, I recommend that you try not to tackle all of the advice in one sitting. If you do, you'll tire yourself, and you could dilute the message. Instead, absorb the advice in an unrushed but comfortable speed, by reading a few chapters at a time, in any order you wish—since they are not in any particular building-block or sequential order. And should you discover that you are already living by some of the principles, reward yourself today: Indulge yourself in a good novel, enjoy a hot date with your wife tonight, or get tickets for you and a buddy to go to a game this week!

Life's peaks and valleys can take a brother for a loop sometimes. They can leave him feeling clueless as to where to seek solace, reveal his struggles, express his dreams, his anger, his pain. I hope *What Black Men Should Do Now* in some way speaks to you personally, and assures you that there are other brothers just like you who are searching for answers. The words on these pages may serve as a wake-up call for some, while providing other brothers with a compass to reclaim their lives through healing old wounds, restoring self-confidence, or building character. Men going through their midlife crisis may find solace and gain comfort from them. Mature teen brothers may experience "light-bulb moments" from them. Still, for others, the words may provide them with the reinforcement needed to continue living life to its maximum potential. I firmly believe there is something here for men of every age—the young, the "seasoned," and those who fall somewhere in between.

The one hundred strategies that make up this book can spark extraordinary, and necessary dialogue for proud, strong brothers willing to lean on and learn from each other—something we've got to do more of as we shape our purpose on this planet. For this reason, I urge you to share the words on these pages with every brother you know— your father, your son, your brother, your grandfather, your uncle, your cousin, your nephew, your partner, your frat, your best friend.

Action Steps have been provided to complement each of the one hundred strategies. These "action items" are simple, and ones you can implement almost immediately. The Action Steps work in tandem with the strategies themselves to serve as a navigational aid to point you in the direction of living an authentic, centered, and mindful life. By no means are they meant to make up an exhaustive compilation. I have merely presented a smorgasbord of them to give you a head start in generating your own personal "should-do" list. By the nature of their diversity, I guarantee that they will enlighten you, empower you, and get you "thinking outside the box." However, you must be willing to uncross your arms, open your mind, and let them speak to you.

To enhance your reading experience, I suggest "bookending" your day by recording in a journal or logging thoughts from your personal reflections, meditations, and self-discoveries. Incorporate this activity into your daily "me time"— perhaps as you sip your morning brew, or just before you turn out the lights at night. Your journal is also a great place to record the many new and exciting kernels of wisdom you will harvest as a result of talking with other brothers about the strategies presented here. You will find that your written entries will help you track the progress you have made on your journey to becoming your best self and living your best life.

To the women who read this book, I say *What Black Men Should Do Now* is a timeless gift to give to the black men in your life—those you care about and love. As a gift to my brothers, I challenge you to: release your anger; be mentors; be grateful; help to keep the women in your life healthy; practice nonviolence; be a *real* man; have a vision; have a passion; reconnect with your dad; hug your children; take care of your body; remember your spirit; show some affection; and live your wildest dream!

Finally, know that as you are reading, digesting, and practicing the strategies, *I, too,* will be working to apply them to my life, since self-maintenance is a lifelong process. Working together, we can "flip the script" on the life of black men. Together, we can make a difference.

It's been said we pass through only once on this challenging journey called life, but if we work it right, once will be enough. May we all be healthy, wise, and rich in spirit along the way!

ACKNOWLEDGMENTS

No matter what accomplishments you make, somebody helps you.

—Althea Gibson

During the course of my researching, writing, molding and realizing the dream of this book, a colossal network of family, friends, industry experts, creative colleagues and behind-the-scenes forces supported me and embraced *What Black Men Should Do Now* as if it were the most important book on earth. I want to thank and acknowledge that support, creative energy, love, inspiration, guidance, wisdom, faith and honesty so generously given me as I followed my passion and lived one of my own wildest dreams.

First and foremost, I extend gratitude beyond words to the Creator for entrusting me with *What Black Men Should Do Now*. It took a while, but I finally got it; it now makes sense: The reason there had not been a book like this for brothers is that it was reserved for me to produce, and, in turn, grow as a man from the challenge of the experience. Even through all the unknowns and uncertainties of bringing the book to life, He faithfully assured me, "I got your back!" all the way to the bookshelf. The hurdles were many, but in the end, the timing of its release into the world was right. Talk about divine intention!

I owe a tremendous debt of gratitude to all the bright, bold, and resilient black men who opened their hearts and souls to me as I researched this book. Your insights were keen and necessary. And it would not have been possible for me to write knowledgeably about some of the things I did without the personal stories you bravely shared and the wisdom you imparted. Also, to the bright, bold, and beautiful black women who told me their stories and provided insight from their perspective: I thank you for giving me an earful! And many thanks to the quoted men and women whose inspiring words appear on these pages. Their wisdom can provide hope, comfort, and empowerment to all who absorb it. As the French essayist Michel de Montaigne put it, "I quote others only in order to better to express myself."

A heartfelt thanks to family: Allene Oglesby (who reads all my manuscripts—and would have made one heck of a book editor!) and Kenneth Oglesby, my wonderful parents, for a lifetime of love, and unwavering support through all my endeavors; thank you for your presence in my life. I hope I always make you proud to call me your son. And to my sisters Leslie Johnson and Marilyn Oglesby, thank you, too, for your love and support—it means the world! Also, much appreciation to Vivian Bush; Yvette Bush; Dollie Hairston; Gladys Hylton, Pauline Jordan; Vincent Jordan; Shawn McIntyre; Donna Oglesby; Karen Oliver; Mary Pringle; Sarah Pringle-Lewis; Al and Linda Raymond (Thanks for your soothing presence, Linda!); Verbena Reed; Bill Rogers; Alexandra Rucker; Cheryl Rucker; Gg Rucker; David Stackhouse; Beverly Stackhouse; Greg Wood; and members of the Travis-Pringle Society for rooting for me, being at all those book events, setting up and hosting some of those book events, transporting me from here to there, and praying for nothing short of the best for me and the book.

Although this is the book I was born to write, sadly my grandmother, Edith Oglesby—who is always with me in spirit, and would have cherished it dearly—did not live to read it. May *What Black Men Should Do Now* be a loving remembrance.

Well, Aristotle, your secret readings of the book paid off,

because you have remarkably exhibited loyalty and the inexhaustible patience of Job. Good boy! Now, go grab your ball, and let's head to the park to play—play hard! And to my Mt. Olive Baptist Church "family" in Dayton, Ohio, thank you all for your support. I love you all very much!

Most particularly, I give a very special acknowledgment to the following personal friends who through their eternal interest in my writing and professional welfare and constructive critiques helped an idea become a manuscript, and a manuscript a book: Wendy Bailey (my favorite "Moody Reader"); Rick Blalock (with whom I collaborated on my very first book a few years ago, and am currently hard at work with on our next); Karen Celestan; Dr. Grace Cornish (a guerrilla marketer and walking reference source of industry contacts); Cheryl Cosey; E. Lynn Harris (for every moment of writer's inspiration, from the day our paths crossed all those years ago); William July II; Ed Marshall (for your presence); Herman "Skip" Mason Jr.; Victoria Christopher Murray (for your priceless industry advice); Alfred Washington; and Malik Marc-Levy Williams. These, too, are the people who, like me, knew that what I dubbed as "The Little Book That Could" had to be and would be put out into the universe— no matter what it took. Thanks, guys, for believing and for being my rock.

I am blessed to have six of the most wonderful longtime friends who are always with me in spirit: DeLena Aungst, Rob Hanselman, Craig Lewis, Bennie McRae, and Denny and Edie Volz. I appreciate you and the years of support you've given. And I'm honored to have you in my life.

The esteemed Dr. Rosie Milligan of Milligan Books, thank you for giving me my book-writing start, and pushing me onward and upward. Words cannot express the deep sense of love and appreciation I have for you. I am blessed to have been one of the many whose author's career you've launched. You're simply the best!

And Tavis (Smiley), I can't thank you enough, man, for your interest in and support of this project from the second day our paths crossed and I shared it with you. My friend, you are definitely helping to make black America better through your empowering words and tireless campaigns to give empowerment and encouragement to our people. We need a hundred more like you, brotherman. May you always be there, pushing and inspiring us to "keep the faith!"

To fellow writers and new friends Chrisena Coleman; Lolita Files; Nancy Flowers Wilson; Denene Milner; Timmothy B. McCann; Eric E. Pete; Karen Quinones Miller; and Carl Weber: Thank you for your "been-there-done-that-and-this-is-what-you-need-to-do" sage wisdom. Your invaluable words have made a mark. You guys inspire me to keep forging ahead in the unpredictable world of publishing.

It has long been my dream to write a book that would help direct people on the path to being their best selves, and in turn, living their best lives—especially my fellow black brothers and the sisters who love and care about them. This is why I extend a grateful thanks to every person who purchased a copy of the first (hardcover) edition of this book. More than you can know, I especially appreciate your telling all your friends, family members and colleagues to "Buy this book!" and go out and support this brother during all the dates on the national book tour. It's because of you that the book climbed its way to bestseller lists—no one else—and for that I am more than appreciative. All the readings, signings, discussions, and one-on-ones have been as engaging as they are enlightening—not to mention so much fun! I look forward to many more interactions with you for years to come.

There is one entity that without its existence, this book would never have soared to the success it has: the bookstores—especially the African-American booksellers, who hand-sell it when folks walk in the door. I dare not attempt to list them all; however I am compelled to publicly acknowledge particular ones (and the individuals who are the force behind them): Sharon Kelly Roth of Books & Company in Kettering, Ohio, who I call the "Book-Event Omnipotence!"; Cindy Miller and Shaunna McManaway of Waldenbooks-Salem Mall in Trotwood, Ohio (I'm still reeling from the lavish promotion and hand-selling you did—and still do—for this forever grateful hometown boy!); Ken Bates of B. Dalton Bookseller-South DeKalb Mall in Atlanta; and Barnes & Noble Booksellers-Buckhead in Atlanta (Thanks for your eagerness to always host my books' debuts to launch the tours!). And Nia Damali of Medu Bookstore in Atlanta; Emma Rodgers of Black Images Book Bazaar in Dallas; Gigi Roane of Drum & Spear Bookstore in Washington, DC; and Rosie Milligan of Express Yourself Books in Los Angeles, thanks to each of you for the tireless efforts to promote the book, but most of all for your steadfast friendship! And Robin Green-Carey of Sibanye, Inc. in Baltimore, you are a beautiful spirit, sister, and I am honored to know you! I appreciate all you have done for me and the book.

Personal thank-yous to the following media entities for having me as a guest on your shows: Frank Ski, Tara Thomas, and the entire "Frank Ski in the Morning" crew at V-103 FM in Atlanta; Mildred Gaddis of WCHB-1200 AM in Detroit; Bea Thompson of WBAV-101.9 FM in Charlotte; Sandi Mallory of Morgan State University's WEAA-88.9 FM in Baltimore; "Mo" Caradine at WVON-1450 AM in Chicago; WROU-92.1 FM in Dayton, Ohio; and my friends at KISS-104.1 FM in Atlanta.

I also want to thank my journalist friends and colleagues for their friendship and media-appearance assistance. In Dayton, Ohio: Marsha Bonhart of WDTN-TV *2News*; Letitia Perry of WHIO-TV *Newscenter 7*; and in New Orleans: Monica Pierre of WQUE-93 FM. You're three strong sisters who have it goin' on, and I'm proud to know you! Also, big thank-yous to the following for all their media-assistance:

Dionne Butler of WWL-TV 4 *Eyewitness News* in New Orleans; Shirley Washington of *FOX4* in Dallas; Ken Watts and Leslie Betty of WXIA-TV 11 *11Alive* News in Atlanta; Mashaun D. Simon of the *Atlanta Daily World;* Gregory Lee of *The Washington Post;* Stan Washington of the *Atlanta Voice; Ebony* magazine; *Black Issues Book Review;* Tangie Black of *GN* magazine; and *Belle* magazine.

Many thanks to Thomas Dortch, Jill Bell, and the members of 100 Black Men of America; and to Harry Johnson Sr. and the members of Alpha Phi Alpha Fraternity, for inviting me to participate in your literary events at your annual conventions. I can't think of more appropriate audiences than these two—and I had the best time! And much love to the Atlanta Association of Black Journalists for your staunch support through the years.

Great appreciation to a close circle of people for going well beyond the call of duty in showing unyielding love and support to a friend. You've been at the book events again and again, told all your friends, family members and colleagues about all the book events, purchased tons of copies for yourselves and those you love and care about, helped to generate mega publicity, and pulled many strings to make good things happen! I can't think of how I'll ever repay you: Becky Bartelme (my "biggest fan"—and yes, Beck, you're still going with me on *The Oprah Winfrey Show!*); Dionna Bolar; John Campbell; Tony Dodson; Marsha Eaglin; Joyce Fleming; Deon Fletcher; John Heisey; Betsy Helgager (the PR guru!); Beverly Isom; Le'Son Ivory; Marjorie Ivy; Lois Jackson and the late Luther Jackson; Harold Littlejohn; Carmella Marshall; Jean Maye; Norris Minter; Neil Mapp; Evelyn Mims; Lou Nettles; Andrew Oyefesobi; Alyce Palmer; Daryl Parker; Grafton and Bernice Payne; Clint Preston; Annie Robinson; Vanessa Sawyer; David Smalls; Greg Smalls; Tony Tyms; James Webber (you need not spend another dime buying copies of this book—even if it *is* the new and expanded edition!); Belinda West; GregAlan Williams; Judie Woods; and John Yeiser. Stick around for the next book experience, folks—I'm gonna need ya!

A very special thanks to Denelle Eads, a kindred spirit and lifelong friend who has always been there to cheer me on.

Trè Maxie and Vern Cambridge of MaxXed-Out Entertainment are two of the best in the author/book publicity business, especially when it comes to booking many of those radio- and TV-show appearances. They are first-class, energetic, professional go-getters, and they were always there escorting and coaching to ensure my appearances were the wonderful experiences that they were. Fellas, I can't thank you enough for everything you did for me in the way you did it! I also give a standing ovation to the staff at 21st Century Communications. I don't know how *What Black Men Should Do Now* would have come to be without these two entities. I know it was grueling work promoting this one, but from the remarkable response of reading black America, it paid off in too many ways to count.

A special thank-you to photographer David Stembridge for the looks you created for my publicity shots for this and my last book. The shoot was a lot of fun, and you're a man of sheer talent! And Tony Coleman deserves thanks for his quiet, but key, support.

A big thank-you to my friend Ricky Boyd, who gave me my professional start and sparked my interest in preserving the health and social well-being of African-American men. You're a pioneer to be celebrated! And special thanks to my former manager, mentor and friend Bill Wharton, one of the smartest men I know! When I was a communications rookie, you took the time to teach, push, and encourage me toward perfection; that guidance and wisdom has followed me throughout my career. For that, I will always be grateful.

My hope was to find an agent and an editor to share my vision and passion for this book. I did. When I needed an agent, my friend and talented author Felicia Mason (Thanks, Felicia!) steered me in the right direction to Linda Hyatt, who shepherded the project from start to finish. My dynamic original editor Monica Harris, who watched over the first edition of *What Black Men Should Do Now*, is a rare find who one can only dream of working with. These three ladies hung right in there with me, through all the bizarre twists and turns of this book's journey, and I'll always remember and feel blessed by their fortitude.

Much gratitude to the entire Kensington team, for believing in this book and making me feel like family at my new publishing home! I am especially grateful beyond belief to Karen Thomas, my new editor, who wholeheartedly embraced and breathed new life into this book through Kensington's awesome Dafina imprint. Karen, you have been a Godsend! And Bruce Bender, you took good care of me during the book's midstream transition from one house to another. The tremendous contributions you have made helped to make the ride smoother. Know that Thanksgiving week 2000—when I held the book in my hands for the first time— will always be a memorable moment for me. Jessica McLean-Ricketts at Kensington is a jewel for keeping sales up and the book stocked in stores!

Next, I thank the editors of the Black Expressions Book Club for selecting my and Monica's "baby" as an Alternate Featured Selection of the month. I am honored to be included in the company of so many other talented authors, many of whom have mentored me and served as role models for me.

Jane Dystel of Jane Dystel Literary Management, thank you for coming along at the right time. I'm pleased as all getout to be represented by an agent extraordinaire! I look forward to working on projects galore to come!

Music moves and inspires me, especially when I am writing late at night through the wee hours of the morning— which is usually the case. And the tunes of certain artists seem to soothe and push out with ease the words from my head onto the computer keyboard, then onto the computer screen. They don't know it, but the following people's musical talents are instrumental to my writing: Natalie Cole, Miles Davis, Earth, Wind & Fire, Billie Holiday, James Ingram, Elton John, Diana Krall, Aaron Neville, Joshua Redmond, Seal, James Taylor, Tina Turner, Grover Washington Jr., Cassandra Wilson, and Nancy Wilson. Thank you, for every musical moment.

Finally, I bow down to the ancestors in gratitude for their passion, which fueled my own.

Clearly, I have many people to thank, and I hope and pray I have not omitted anyone. For those I have, know that it was not intentional. For those friends, family members, colleagues and a multitude of others who remain unnamed, you know I recognize the all-important loving, nurturing and supporting roles you have played (and continue to play) in my writing adventures and in my life. I am indebted to you, too, well beyond words.

WHAT BLACK MEN
SHOULD DO NOW

1. Ac-cent-chu-ate the positive.

To be a great champion, you must believe you are the best.
If you're not, pretend you are.

—Muhammad Ali, humanitarian and former
heavyweight boxing champion

Every morning you decide the type of day you will have. You can make it a great one, or you can make it a horrible one—it's up to you. No one can make you sad. No one can make you glad. You determine your own emotional state. No one else has a say. Now, that's a lot of power!

Intelligent brothers exercise their right to that power. They milk it for all it's worth! They make every day a great day, because they remain cognizant of the fact that there are already enough ills contributing to their plight as black men in this country—homicide, AIDS, racism, and cancer, just to name a few. They see no rhyme or reason for consciously inviting additional negatives—drugs, jealous mates, back-stabbing "friends," abusive parents, sometimey family members, bad debt—into their lives. They live with optimism and gratitude. They have a pep in their step, a stride in their glide. They walk by faith, radiate with certitude. They're always mindful that the best is yet to come, and it has their name written all over it! Optimistic and upbeat people make a conscious decision to tune out the naysayers and keep the evil spirits at bay. Not with sticks. Not with salt. And certainly not with garlic! Rather, they possess good thoughts,

3

connect with good vibes, stay prayerful, and surround themselves with good people aspiring to good things.

Certainly, all of us in our lifetime, will experience times of hardships and doubts. We will have to face wave after wave of discouragement, disillusionment, and displeasure. This is a part of life, and life is not always fair—we know that. Genuine, positive people are realistic: They don't view the world through rose-colored glasses, but with 20-20 vision. They realize that the earth and its people are indeed flawed, but they choose to accentuate the good things, providing them with spectacular benefits: better health, more energy, creativity, better problem-solving abilities, the facility to hang in there, and an overall sense of happiness.

As black men, let us collectively *ac-cent-chu-ate* the positives *and e-li-mi-nate* the negatives from our lives. Heaven knows, as people of color, we have no use for "Mr. In-Between." Remember, you are part of a blessed, proud, and strong race, comprised of loving, caring, and resilient black men. We are capable of choosing the roads we travel on the journey of life. Therefore, we must choose those roads wisely and make them work for us.

The aptness to maintain a positive mental attitude is a self-imposed skill we all should be empowered to possess—and be adept at it. Resolve today to let yesterday's negatives go, and march on toward becoming the most positive-and-enthu-siastic-about-life person you know! Then spread it around—it's contagious!

Action Steps

- Make it second-nature to keep positive thoughts in your mind at all times—particularly during challenging moments that test your patience, faith, and endurance. Taking good care of your emotional and physical self will change the way you look at life—and ultimately change how you live it!

- Realize that putting a limit on what you will do puts a limit on what you *can* do.
- Surround yourself with positive people doing positive things. Then bask in the glow!
- When negative folks start talkin' their talk, politely turn the conversation around by saying something positive, and keep the conversation flowing in that direction.
- Refuse to sanction self-pitying attitudes in others.
- Take inventory of all the good things that have happened in your life in the last month. Write them down, and be grateful for them.
- Find the silver lining when things seem cloudy and gray. It's there—you may just need to search a little. Keep in mind, what doesn't kill you will make you stronger and wiser.
- Exercise the power of thinking B-I-G, and you will achieve all you aim for!

2. Don't be an "angry black man."

> . . . I have had—and have—my own pain . . . from
> racism to poverty to brokenness and it is the struggle of
> day-to-day living. . . . Pain can make us bitter or better. I
> wanted to be made better.
>
> —T. D. Jakes, Christian bishop and author

People of color have been through a lot in this country. Discrimination, racism, unemployment, miseducation, and violence have been constants for many African Americans. Yet we have endured. This is particularly true for the black man, who continues to feel the brunt of many societal ills. Some brothers are bitter. Can you blame them? Well, in reality, we don't have time to be bitter.

For some men, anger has become a way of life. They know

no other way. However, a man who rises at dawn with anger, rage, and resentment aimed at "the Man" or "the System" cheats himself; he does not experience a completely settled mind, inner peace, and contentment with his place in the world.

Harboring angry feelings deep within our hearts does not help to solve the ills we have suffered because of the skin color we bear. It brings only turmoil to the mind of the man who is highly capable of righting the wrongs, changing "the System," and enlightening "the Man" through positive actions and a loving heart.

No, we will never forget the hundreds of years of blood, sweat, and tears that were shed as we were traded, sold, put to stud, and bred like animals. It's unrealistic to even *think* we would forget—we have been through too much. Although our civil-rights efforts during the fifties and sixties brought many changes, such as the right to vote, and later, affirmative action programs, many of those gains are now being vociferously challenged. We continue to be followed closely by suspicious clerks in department stores, pulled over for DWB (driving while black), and denied country-club memberships—even after Tiger Woods won two Masters tournaments.

Yes, "the System" still needs work. "the Man" still needs enlightening; and we still get angry. However, deep-rooted anger must not be what guides our psyche or lives. If we let it, we will surely self-destruct as individuals and as a community. As survivors, let us turn away from pointless hatred, and toward positive constructive actions.

Not until there is a shift in social consciousness will we see a complete erasure of racism and discrimination. The haul may be long, and the cross we bear may be heavy. However, with clear minds, a desire to enlighten, warm hearts, and positive attitudes, our journey will be shorter and lighter.

Action Steps

- Get mad, then try to change "the System."

- Get mad, then get over it. Life is too short to waste your time and energy on its negative aspects.

- When you think you have hit rock bottom, remember, there's nowhere to go but up.

- Use your wallet, expertise, or determination, not violence, as a means to effect change.

3. Have the courage to cry when you are sad.

We have been raised to never shed a tear no matter how it hurts. We can be better men if we understand that it's all right at certain moments in our life to shed a tear.

—M. C. Hammer, entertainer

Far too many black men are walking around in emotional pain, suffering in silence. At some point in our history, we fellas were conditioned to hide our emotions—particularly emotions that may result in tears of sadness. We go to the greatest lengths to "suck it up" and hold back those tears. "Naw, man, I'm all right. I'm cool," are often the first words out of our mouths when we feel emotions building, especially when other men are present. Brothermen, we must not be afraid to let others see us cry.

Unfortunately, society deems happiness and anger as somewhat acceptable emotions for a brother to show. Crying is *not* a sign of weakness—it's part of being human. Think back to a time when you saw another man cry. Perhaps it was your father. Your granddaddy. Your buddy. Or maybe your boss. Was it at a funeral of a loved one? Or maybe it was during a joyous occasion—graduation, confirmation, or during the birth of a child. Sometimes seeing another man cry makes you feel helpless, not knowing what to do to comfort him. Surely you do not condemn him for crying. Rather, a warm, brotherly embrace may be just what he needs to let him know you care.

While we work to become more comfortable with expressing our own emotions, we also need to tell our sons, nephews, and the young boys we mentor that big boys *do* cry, and that doing so does not make them weak. The Bible recounts how Jesus wept during his most trying moments as a man on earth. In the eyes of many, He has a long-standing reputation for being the strongest brother with whom we are familiar.

So, as strong brothers, let us be in touch with our spectrum of feelings, from joy to sadness, fear to anger. The shedding of tears can be an experience of ultimate release. It enables the mightiest man to feel renewed, whether it is to let go of guilt, cleanse his heavy heart, forgive himself, or finally begin to heal.

Action Steps

- Never tell a child—especially a young brother—"Big boys don't cry." We do—and it's okay.
- Don't be afraid to show your emotions in front of your mate, children, or friend. No one will condemn you for it. When your heart is heavy, that person may be just the pillar of strength you need to lean on.
- Know that you don't have to hold on to the pain.

4. Uphold the African-American woman.

I am convinced that the black man will only reach his full potential when he learns to draw upon the strengths and insights of the black woman.

—Manning Marable, director of the Institute for Research in African American Studies and professor of history, Columbia University

For the African-American woman, "life ain't been no crystal stair. It had tacks in it. And splinters. And boards torn up," as the poet Langston Hughes wrote.

Since her arrival to the New World, she has endured it all—from rape and the auctioning of her babies to menial labor, as well as the "blackout" in Hollywood, in the boardroom, and in the pulpit.

When we disrespect our sisters with hatred, abuse, and call them names like "bitch," "hootchie," "tramp," and "ho," we kill the team spirit our people have used since arriving on these shores from the Motherland four hundred years ago. If you were a woman, how would you feel if you were the object of such humiliation and degradation? Our women are on our side, brothers. Don't alienate them; we can't afford it. For their blood, too, pumps through the veins of the virile legs we lift to climb our own splintered staircase.

Brotherman, remember this about the sister:

She is lovable. Love her.
She is beautiful. Flaunt her.
She is intelligent. Learn from her.
She is sexy. Experience her.
She is delicious. Taste her.
She is soft. Cuddle with her.
She is an asset. Take stock in her.
She is meaningful. Cherish her.

She is sensitive. Comfort her.

She is priceless. Value her.

She is a gem. Reflect on her.

She is radiant. Bask in her.

She is strong. Gain strength from her.

She is deep. Seek to understand her.

She is striking. Stand in awe of her.

She is "all that." Be impressed by her.

She is funny. Laugh with her.

She is giving. Share with her.

She is spiritual. Worship with her.

She is forgiving. Seek forgiveness from her.

She is human . . . Expect that from her.

Let us collectively uphold our sisters with the same respect we ask of them for us.

Action Steps

- Next time you hear a brother dis a woman, rather than cheer him on, call him on it.
- Establish a rule of not allowing people to put others down in your home, at the workplace, or anywhere else. Put them on notice that you prefer to surround yourself with positives.

5. Go to the doctor to get regular health checkups.

You can be afraid of needles all day long, but you can still give blood at the doctor's office. But when somebody says, "Lie down on the table. I'm going to stick this tube in you," they say "[No], I feel great." They're just not educated [people].

—Eric Davis, major-league baseball player, who successfully had a cancerous tumor removed

During a visit to his doctor's office, John was told something that confirmed what he had read about recently: Generally speaking, black men do not go to the doctor.

As she checked his vital signs, the African-American nurse told John: "It's good to see a black man coming in for his annual checkup. You know, my husband is thirty-two years old, and he's never even had a physical. I've tried to get him in here so many times, but he'd have to be carried in on a stretcher just to get him to see a doctor."

One would think that the husband of this nurse who works with a black male doctor would heed his wife's urgings. However, the nurse's story is not uncommon. Many women have to fight tooth and nail just to get their stubbornly reluctant or even scared man to make an appointment—let alone go—to see a doctor. What's more, some men don't even have a regular physician to visit for simple aches and pains.

Unlike women, who tend to visit the doctor's office regularly, men (not just black men) are hesitant to seek medical attention. Many of us see doing so as admitting weakness. Fact is, going to the doctor on a regular basis is one of the most intelligent things we can do for ourselves. In the process, we can save those we love and care about from unnecessary anguish, suffering, and even grief.

Unlike our cars, we do not come with warranties, fellas.

Ours is the only body we get. When the body runs its course, we don't trade it in, we junk it. So let's do the proper maintenance to ward off our extremely high incidences of hypertension, cancer, AIDS, and cardiovascular disease.

It's time to change our attitudes about our bodies. We have to protect them through education, early detection, and treatment. Although it's smart to see the doctor when we're sick and trying to get better, we must also see one when we are healthy. When we do this, we will ensure we are truly the "well-oiled machines" we like to boast we are.

Action Steps

- Don't let a preventable illness strike before you begin seeing a doctor. It may be too late.

- Choose a physician with whom you are comfortable. To make an informed choice, make appointments with several prospective doctors to meet and talk with them for ten minutes or so. Consider your doctor as your ally, one who is there to help.

- A few years ago, director-actor Spike Lee urged African Americans to "Do the right thing!" as a spokesperson for the National Cancer Institute's campaign to fight cancer. Let's continue to heed his warning and get the facts about testicular cancer. Your local health department or doctor's office should have pamphlets about it.

- If you have been diagnosed with diabetes, understand that you don't just have a "touch of sugar," brother—you have *diabetes*! Call it what it is, and treat it for what it is: an illness to be well-managed and not to be taken lightly. For more information, call the American Diabetes Associations' African American Program at 1-800-DIABETES (342-2383).

- Do a monthly testicular self-exam. The check is quick, easy, painless, and effective—but not nearly enough of us do it. Testicular cancer is the most common type of tumor diagnosed in men between the ages of twenty and thirty-five. Here's the good news: While the disease cannot be prevented, if detected early its cure can be effective—at higher rates than any other type of cancer (95 percent). Your doctor's office or local health department should be able to give you a testicular self-exam shower hanger (a plastic water-resistant die-cut card that hangs on the showerhead). On the card are simple instructions for a self-exam.

- Always follow your doctor's order "to a T"—whether it is to finish all the prescribed medicine, attend physical therapy sessions, kick a cigarette habit, or abstain from sexual intercourse.

- Attend health fairs, conferences, and seminars on African-American health.

- Remember, your sons, nephews, grandsons, and male cousins should begin seeing their own doctors at age eighteen.

- Add the book *The Black Man's Guide to Good Health,* by James W. Reed, Charlene Shucker, and Neil B. Shulman, to your personal home library.

6. Don't have sex, make love.

Sex is when you don't give a damn. Making love is when you care.

—Barry White, entertainer

Sho' you right, Barry!

How many times have we heard our partners urge us to "Slow down, baby," "Wait a minute," and "No—don't move! Don't move!" in the heat of our most intimate moments with them?

Men generally feel we must conquer and achieve in everything we do—in fact, we are socialized that way in our early years. As adults, we carry this notion into the bedroom. And too often we race toward the "finish line" without taking time to savor the sweet journey of foreplay along the way. We'd never admit it, but we fellas often feel the need to perform in between the sheets with our lovers, asserting a lion-like prowess just before our climactic "conquering" roar of liberation.

Well, guess what. In our need to feel desirable and uninhibited during sex, we must be willing to share in every ounce of passion with our partners. Sex is sacred. Sex is natural. Sex should be fun. Let us relax our egos and learn to let go during lovemaking. When we are busy putting on a show, we cheat our partners and ourselves out of all that our intense moment has to offer. We don't want that—we might miss something.

Great lovers are made, not born. So, next time, relax, let go, slow down. You're not onstage. And no one's on a stopwatch. All this will come naturally if you're making love. The experience is guaranteed to bring you all the romping pleasures that make you glad you're a man!

Action Steps

- Know that you don't always have to be "in the driver's seat." Let your lover drive sometimes; you navigate, providing the directions to all the hot spots.

- Know that you are not a failure if your wife or mate doesn't always climax during lovemaking. Accept it. Women and men are "wired" differently. Respect her enough to ask her what she wants and needs to be satisfied in the relationship.

- Love yourself enough to tell your mate what you want and need under the covers.

- Has sex between the two of you become monotonous or routine? Talk with your mate about ways to intensify the emotional connection between you—in and outside the bedroom.

- Have you and/or your partner lost complete desire for making love with each other? Be a man about it by initiating the conversation on why, and then suggest seeking the professional help of a sex therapist and/or marriage counselor. Therapy *can* help.

7. Volunteer in your community.

It's time to shift our focus to Main Street, where the real work awaits us. We cannot hope to achieve our goal of reaching two million youngsters at a stroke. It can only be achieved one community at a time, one street at a time, and one child at a time.

—Gen. Colin Powell, USA (ret.),
U.S. Secretary of State

Brother Powell, who heads up the national volunteerism initiative America's Promise, the Alliance for Youth, couldn't be more right. We can all do our part to help turn the tide. There is no greater service we can render than helping people who need help. It doesn't cost anything except time. Every day you get a new twenty-four-hour clock—use it!

Volunteering can be one of the most rewarding experiences of a lifetime. Former president Jimmy Carter was once asked why he volunteered so often. He replied by saying that volunteering his services allowed him to witness different walks of life that he might not have otherwise known. We can never learn enough, and by volunteering we can reap the the same benefit that Carter does.

Remember this, too: Every helping hand helps. Don't sit back and think that others can—or should—carry the load. Somewhere down the line, someone carried a load for you. You may not have known him or realized it, but someone volunteered to help you in some way or another. Plus, if you have any belief in "what goes around, comes around," then imagine what's in store for you if you take time out to help someone.

There are thousands of ways to put your volunteer spirit to work—everything from helping the neighbor next door to working in organized groups with directed goals and objectives. Consider assisting Boys and Girls Clubs, local Ys, or school and community groups, just to name a few.

Think about it. If we all pitch in, we can make a better world for the next generation.

Action Steps

- Tired of the inner cities' harsh effects on young black boys? Work with at-risk youths who may not value all the gifts of life.
- Good with your hands, tools, and making repairs? Lend your talent to the group effort of building a new house for someone less fortunate by joining Habitat for Humanity.
- Good at giving advice? Volunteer with a crisis hotline project.
- Comfortable with speaking to groups of people? Teach violence-prevention and/or mediation to adults and children.
- Good with the elderly? Spend time with them at a retirement home, community nursing home, or senior citizens' center on your day off.
- Excelling in your career? Don't just tell, *show* other brothers (young and old) they can do it too.

8. Be a mentor and a role model to a young brother.

A mentor is always there, telling a child to believe: To believe in himself or herself, to believe in the opportunities that are available and above all, to believe in their dreams. It is the adults who pass that on to the next generation.

—Janet Jackson, entertainer

There can never be enough positive role models for young boys, especially African-American boys. With so much media attention focused on bad images of black men and other people of color, it is vital that successful black men step up to the plate.

Sure, many young brothers have a hero they look up to, like Michael Jordan or Tiger Woods. They not only idolize their heroes, they often imitate them. However, our boys need someone they can touch and talk to in person. Whether you are a sanitation engineer who lives down the block, or a schoolteacher in the classroom, you can play a part. You have the power to help steer a young life on the right path. You possess the ability to make a difference because these young brothers can know you.

Remember, when we mentor in our community, we feel better not only about the prospects of the race, but also about ourselves. It's exciting to know you helped to turn a life around. Being the wind beneath a child's wings lends to a feeling inside that invigorates the soul. Furthermore, when we mentor, we help keep one more kid off the streets and out of trouble, and prevent one more tragedy from becoming the day's headline. Also, we offer young people a chance to experience a new perspective on life—something outside of their everyday environment. Today, choose to make a difference.

Action Steps

- Join a group whose mission is to help young people, such as Big Brothers Big Sisters.

- Volunteer to work with young people during after-school activities.

- Spend quality time with children in the neighborhood. Teach them to ride a bike, fish, play Scrabble, build a tree house, use a computer, or paint.

- If golf is your game, teach young people how to play. Take them to the course or to the driving range for a few free lessons.

- Think of the man or woman who mentored you. Call him or her today to say thanks for making a difference in your life. You'll both be glad you did.

- To find out more about how you can be a mentor to a young person, call 1-888-55–YOUTH. Also visit these Web sites: America's Promise, the Alliance for Youth Web at http://www.americaspromise.org and the National Mentoring Partnership at http://www.mentoring.org/

9. Practice nonviolence.

We must turn to each other and not on each other.
—The Rev. Jesse Jackson, civil-rights leader

One thing many brothers know about is violence in our community. Some of us have been a victim of it, or witnessed it firsthand, while others have heard it, or read about it. Violence is something that has touched most of our lives in some way or another. It comes in many forms—physical abuse, mental abuse, even yelling, arguing, and cursing. Violence often occurs between two acquaintances or two people who know each other well. It can be our brothers, mothers, grandfathers, friends, or coworkers who are involved in the conflict.

Black males are statistically implicated in only a small percentage of the number of violent crimes in America, yet we are more likely to appear on the front page of a daily newspaper or at the top of the newscast as a result of illegal activities, than if we have done something positive in the community. Indeed, we grow weary as we hear about another three or four black men in our community being murdered. Unfortunately murder is the fourth leading cause of death for all black men. It is the leading cause of death for black males between the ages of fifteen and twenty-four.

It is in our best interest to act quickly to stop the senseless killings, rapes, abuse, and hatred among our people. Our survival depends on it.

Remember, before we point fingers toward the white man for plotting to exterminate us, let us first look at ourselves and question what we are doing to stop killing each other. We don't have to look very far to discover that right now we are doing a fine job at *self*-extermination.

Action Steps

- Never hit your partner or children; remember, clenched fists don't make a man.

- If you must keep a gun in your home, keep it and the bullets in separate places. Also, keep them out of the reach of children.

- Don't be a bully. What goes around comes around, and you'll get yours in the long run.

- If you suspect domestic abuse, report it immediately. Call the National Domestic Violence Hotline at 1–800–799–7233.

- If you suspect a child is being abused, report it by calling Child Help USA National Child Abuse Hotline at 1–800–422–4453.

- Understand what constitutes sexual harassment on and off the job.

- Take a violence-prevention or mediation course offered through a community center or school. Then teach what you have learned to others. You will be amazed by what you will learn about the many faces of violence and how to better handle your own anger.

- Do not yell or cuss at someone to get what you want. Count to ten; take a deep breath; lower your voice, and opt to discuss the matter later, when you are calmer.

10. Exercise regularly.

You can buy all the sports equipment and clothing you want, and you can join a health club, but if the gear stays in the closet, and you don't actually go to the health club, it doesn't do you any good.

—David Satcher, former U.S. Surgeon General

You've heard it before: A healthy body makes for a healthy mind. The two work in tandem. It's called the mind-body connection. But not enough of us take the time to *make* that connection. In today's society, we're all on the go, we stay busy—maybe even too busy to think about fitness. Well, it's time to change our mindset, troops, because when we take good care of our bodies, our bodies take good care of us. This is just another example of the law of the universe called *cause and effect.*

Health and fitness experts say exercise—coupled with a healthy diet—has been scientifically proven to help prevent certain diseases and also promote longer and healthier lives. And as black men, we *have* to take all the necessary precautions against disease, which seems to plague us more than any other ethnic group in this country.

Studies show you can make a huge difference in your well-being by simply spending one hour exercising just three days a week. Activities such as walking, jogging, running, swimming, spinning, skating, dancing, golfing, gardening, mowing the lawn, doing TaeBo, and social dancing all qualify. However, you must augment those three hours with at least twenty minutes of continuous exercise on alternate days. And get this: the National Institute of Mental Health reports that exercise enhances self-esteem, helps you relax and makes sleeping easier, makes you more alert mentally, and lowers anxiety levels. Now, this is good news for brothers!

If you want to be thinner, you've gotta to do more than just back away from the table. If you want to reduce your cholesterol, you must do more than merely eliminate it from your diet. If you want to control (and, in some cases, eliminate certain cases of) your diabetes, you have to do more than just throw out your sugar bowl, take your medicine, and inject your insulin. You've gotta work for those goals. While many men opt to join and hit the local gym to get fit, toned, or even buff, exercising can be done outside the gym too—at home, in a hotel room or hotel exercise facility while you're traveling, in the park, or in your office—all for free! It doesn't cost a dime to drop down and do some pushups, sit up and do some crunches, stand up and do some jumping jacks, and lie back and pump some iron. What's more, staying fit also helps you prevent injury and helps you deal better with stress. (And brothers, you know we know stress!) Belonging to a health club with all the workout amenities and personal trainers is fine, and quite beneficial. However, you don't need fancy equipment or have to wear expensive workout clothes to get fit. You don't need a lot of time, or even have to completely rearrange your life (just a little time-management). All you need is the will to start and the drive to persist.

If you're not active, resolve today to exercise your right to a healthy body and, in turn, a healthy mind. Make this day the day you will change your attitude about physical fitness. Stop viewing it as an optional annoyance, and embrace it as a necessary lifesaver. You're special, brother, and the sisters who love and care about you want you around. At some point today, write out your fitness goals, enlist a workout partner, (to hold you accountable!), be mindful of your diet, and aim to get (as fitness guru Bill Phillips says) a "body for life"!

Action Steps

- If you're thirty or better, always check with your doctor before beginning an exercise or workout program. Follow a routine exercise based on what your physician says.

- Always "warm up" with a good stretching routine just before shocking your body's muscles with the wear and tear that's to come. And don't forget to "cool down" after a workout, to avoid the occurrence of any muscle fatigue, like a cramp; in fact, yoga is an ideal cool-down routine following a tiring workout.

- If you join a health club or gym, join one near your home or workplace to curtail excuses for not going because of lengthy distance and rush-hour traffic.

- Consider hiring a personal trainer to help you make the mind-body connection.

- Exercise with your mate, a good buddy, a family member. Working together can make the experience more fun, and you can keep each other motivated.

- Treat exercising as the lifesaving appointment that it is. Record your workout schedule in your organizer or calendar along with all your other important meetings and engagements.

- This week, subscribe to health and exercise magazines, such as *Men's Exercise* and *Men's Fitness.* Read about new and safe ways to expand your workout routine.

- Read (or listen to the CD audiobook) *Make the Connection,* by Bob Greene and Oprah Winfrey; *BodyChange,* by Montel Williams and Wini Linguvic; and *Body For Life,* by Bill Phillips and Michael D'Orso. They can propel you to change your life!

11. Establish goals and go for them.

> . . . *The tragedy in life doesn't lie in not reaching your goal. The tragedy lies in having no goal to reach. It isn't a calamity to die with dreams unfulfilled, but it is certainly a calamity not to dream. It is not a disaster to be unable to capture your ideal, but it is a disaster to have no ideal to capture.*
>
> —Benjamin E. Mays, former president
> of Morehouse College

Like a coach without a playbook, a man who has no plan has nothing to follow. What game is more important than the game of life?

Goals give us something to shoot for. They help us transform our dreams into reality. Goal-setting encompasses twelve areas of our lives that make up the big picture: personal, spiritual, relationships, family, physical health, mental health, social, career, education, recreation/leisure time, community services, and retirement. While our personal goals usually differ from work-related ones, the two should complement each other in the overall scheme of things. Once we have the big picture fine-tuned the way we want it, we attain better balance in our lives.

Just having goals is not enough, though. You must record them so that you have a tangible, daily reminder of what they are and what your action plan is in order to reach them. You've heard it many times before: "If it's not on paper, it doesn't exist." It's true!

Action Steps

- If you have established goals, examine your present lifestyle and determine if your goals all fit together to balance your life.

- If your life goals are not on paper, write them down—personal and professional ones.

- Develop a personalized strategy to achieve realistic goals.

- Check out the many books on goal-setting at your favorite bookstore or local library. A good title is one that includes an easy step-by-step plan for you to follow.

- When speaking of your aspirations, never say "if"; say "when."

12. Don't bite the hand that feeds you.

Cast no dirt into the well that gives you water.

—Proverb

This was the third time in five days Derrick and Mario's manager Bob needed them to work late at the office. It was "budget time" at the company, which meant the corporate marketing department would not be the only office where desk lamps would burn the midnight oil.

Monday Night Football was also on tonight, and Derrick, who wasn't thrilled about having to stay late again, was very vocal about it. He couldn't understand why, when the budget wasn't due for thirty days, they had to work late this night of all nights.

It didn't matter that the manager rarely asked them to put in overtime. Bob understood that Derrick, Mario, and he himself had wives and children awaiting their arrival at home. As a manager, Bob did not believe in the workaholic philosophy.

This night was critical, however. Bob needed a preliminary budget to submit to his own supervisor in two days. Unlike Mario, who realized the stakes, Derrick sat at his computer terminal with his lower lip poked out, rambling on about how he was going to report Bob for forcing the staff to work overtime without even getting extra pay.

As for Mario, his "stick-to-it-tive-ness," hard work, and commitment paid off. He was later promoted to assistant director of the department and received a hefty bonus after budgets were approved. Derrick, on the other hand, continues what he calls his "daily grind," staying in the same position at the same salary.

Like Derrick, some folks bite the very hand that feeds them. Remember, life is full of give and take. If you take, take, take, and rarely give anything back, you're certain to get very little in return.

Action Steps

- Don't have a negative attitude at work. The people who make the decisions see and hear, and it will not benefit you in the long run.
- Volunteer to help out those in need.
- Make sure you keep open lines of communication in both directions.

13. Practice safer sex—always!

> *You don't want to be like the man on the road, not*
> *believing in the signs. If the sign says, "there's a cliff*
> *ahead" make a turn and believe it. AIDS is for real! . . .*
> *I only need so many examples [to know] that I can't get*
> *away with things like I used to. It has changed my sexual*
> *patterns.*
>
> —Robert Pack, athlete

Safer sex. Learn it. Live it. Teach it. Preach it. There is no such thing as safe sex—only *safer*! Brother, all sex can have consequences—from emotional consequences to diseases and pregnancy. Long before we were introduced to AIDS (Acquired Immunodeficiency Syndrome) in the early 1980s, syphilis was considered a death sentence. Well, it's a new day, brother. We are living in fearful times. During the last few years, the face of people with AIDS has changed drastically— it's now ours, African Americans'. What many black men in this country dismissed as a gay white man's disease has begun to run rampant in the black community.

In August 2001, the Centers for Disease Control and Prevention (CDC) estimated 900,000 people are infected with HIV, one third of whom don't know they have it because they haven't been tested. About 320,000 of those 900,000 have developed AIDS. About 36 million people have HIV—25 million of them in Africa, about eight million in other underdeveloped nations in Asia and India. The majority will develop full-blown AIDS and die. Each year 40,000 people in the U.S. contract the disease. Through June 2000, a total of 753,907 cases of AIDS had been reported to the CDC. What's even more disturbing is that the CDC reports that AIDS continues to be the number-one killer of African Americans between the ages of twenty-five and forty-four. The 1999 rate of reported AIDS cases among African Americans was 66.0 per 100,000 population, more than two times greater than the rate for Hispanics and eight times greater than the rates for whites. A total of 21,000 cases were reported among African Americans, representing nearly half (47 percent) of the 46,400 AIDS cases reported that year. AIDS has replaced homicide as the leading cause of death among young black men. According to a 2001 CDC study, nearly 15 percent of gay and bisexual black men between the ages of 23 and 29 become infected with HIV annually. AIDS researchers report that that infection rate, frighteningly, compares to that of South Africa, where the disease threatens national stability. Brothermen, African Americans make up only *13 percent* of the U.S. population!

Now, if that doesn't disturb you, this ought to: Researchers estimate that one in fifty African-American men are infected with HIV. Sadly, HIV/AIDS became the second leading cause of death for African-American men between the ages of twenty-five and forty-four in 1991; the leading cause of death for African-American women between the ages of twenty-five and forty-four in 1994; and about 58 percent of all children under the age of twelve with AIDS are African American.

While the picture looks bleak, gentlemen, living with (or dying from complications of) AIDS does not have to be the fate of so many of us. Naturally, the best way to protect yourself from AIDS and other sexually transmitted diseases (STDs, or VDs, as we used to call them) and/or the occurrence of an unplanned pregnancy is to practice abstinence. However, for some brothers that is easier said than done. (See strategy number 20: Don't make a baby you're not ready to father.)

Men who cannot commit to abstinence must explore the other option: latex or polyurethane condoms. Using a condom is the best way of preventing disease, but condoms do break, and they are even more likely to break during anal intercourse. Although they are not foolproof, they can be your best bet. Using a condom properly during vaginal and anal sex, and a dental dam or condom during oral sex with your sex partner, is a necessity. A trip to the drugstore to buy "rubbers" is not the embarrassing experience it once was—it is seen as the responsible thing to do. Greater contraceptive protection is possible if contraceptive foams, creams, jellies, films, or suppositories are also used. These products can immobilize sperm if the condom breaks. And some condoms are coated with the spermicide (disinfectant) nonoxynol-9.

Next time you need to pick up a box of "raincoats," for "Johnson," take your partner along with you. Check out the latest assortment of colors, flavors, sizes, and textures on the shelf today. There is something to fit every occasion, from "glow in the dark" and "buck wild" to "bare back" and "sensuously mellow."

So many brothers have moved to a new state: Denial. "It won't happen to me," they think. Fact: Anyone can contract HIV, and as previously stated, there are a number of ways to catch the virus. Many brothers came to that realization in 1991, when former NBA standout Earvin "Magic" Johnson solemnly announced to the world that he is HIV-positive, a result, he says, of his sexual behavior. He later launched his personal campaign to educate others about the disease, which in 2001 marked its twentieth anniversary.

Urgent message to the no-condom-wearing brothers who claim that "rubbers" decrease sensitivity and feeling while "gettin' their hump on": Wake up, and cover your "Johnson!" You're being senseless and reckless with your life! And to "seasoned" brothers age 50+, AIDS does not discriminate: It's an equal-opportunity disease that can grab you too. Regardless of age, race, creed, sex, color, or sexual orientation, if you're not practicing safer sex, it could only be a matter of time before your own visit from the Grim Reaper.

According to the Urban Institute in Washington, young black males between the ages of fifteen and twenty-four are out there having sex like there is no tomorrow—and at the rate they are spreading AIDS, there may be no tomorrow. This group is the least likely of any to use a condom. Black women represent the fastest-growing group with AIDS, and many still won't insist that brothers use a condom.

We're told over and over to communicate to our partners and our children about sex. Yet, when it comes down to it, many of us choke, can't find the courage, won't make the time. We tend to not talk about sex in any kind of realistic way; rather, we joke around it and skim through it. But heart-to-heart conversations are few and far between in the African-American community. Black folks can no longer afford not talking with their partners and children about sex and AIDS. It behooves every brother to get the facts about AIDS.

Remember, you do not have to be bisexual or homosexual to contract the virus. You are strongly urged to get tested if you:

  –had sex with someone who may have been exposed to HIV

  –shared needles or syringes to inject drugs into your body

  –ever contracted an STD

  –had unprotected sex with other males

  –received a blood transfusion or blood products between 1978 and 1985

  –had unprotected sexual activity in the last 10 years with someone whose HIV and *complete* sexual history you did not know at the time of "the act"

–had sex with anyone who could answer yes to any of
the preceding questions

And if it has not been your mode of operation so far, before you "get your swerve on" with anyone else, insist that
you and your prospective partner both have an AIDS test
before getting intimate. Then do the responsible thing and
share your respective results with each other.

Brothers, we have to value the life left in our AIDS-stricken
community by making healthy choices about sex. Our lives
depend on it. Our mates' lives depend on it. Our children's
lives depend on it. When it comes to AIDS, ignorance is not
bliss. Lack of communication and education can mean a
death sentence. Remember, fellas, one unprotected moment
is all it takes, so, put your "thinking caps" on!

Action Steps

- Wait until you are in a monogamous, committed relationship
  before enjoying partner sex. Otherwise, know that the safest
  sex for you is solo sex, brother!

- Educate yourself about HIV/AIDS. Know what's fact and
  what's myth. Places to find out more about the disease include: your local health department, church, public library,
  community AIDS-awareness programs, and on the Internet at
  http://www.cdc.gov; also check out the American Social
  Health Association Web site at http://www.ashastd.org to
  learn not only about AIDS but all other STDs as well.

- For more information, call the CDC National STD and AIDS
  Hotline toll-free at 1-800-342-AIDS (2437), in TTY: 1-800-243-
  7889, or in Español: 1-800-344-7432. Counselors/advisors are
  available to answer your questions twenty-four hours a day,
  seven days a week. They can also give you information on
  anonymous testing sites in your area. (Many state and county

health departments also provide the blood test free for those who cannot afford it.)

- Get answers to your specific questions about herpes from the National Herpes Hotline by calling 1-919-361-8488.

- Visit http://www.condomania.com to check out the hottest new condoms and other fun items on the market today; learn how to properly put on a condom; how to negotiate safer sex with your partner; and get the facts about AIDS and other STDs.

- School yourself. Send off for a free brochure titled "Condoms, Contraceptives, and STDs," that illustrates how to use male and female condoms. Write to: American Social Health Association, P.O. Box 13827, Research Triangle Park, NC 27709, and enclose one dollar to cover postage and handling; or simply call ASHA at 1-800-783-9877 to order the brochure by phone.

- Only use latex condoms—natural-membrane (lamb skin) condoms do *not* protect against sexually transmitted diseases, including HIV. And use only water-based lubricants like K-Y Jelly with them during vaginal and anal intercourse. *Never* use oil-based lubricants like Vaseline, baby oil, lotion, or Crisco—they break down latex rubber and can disintegrate it almost on contact; that's a man-made headache you don't need!

- Never store condoms in your wallet, in the glove compartment of your car, or near heat. Constant exposure to extreme temperature will destroy them.

- Never use a condom more than once. And keep your and your mate's sex toys clean. Infection can set in!

- Don't be surprised if your ladyfriend is prepared and pulls out her *own* stash of condoms—and they may just be female condoms. If you are unfamiliar with how the female condom works, ask her to show you.

- If you are a subscriber, check out America Online's cool "Men's Health" area by going to keyword: MEN'S HEALTH; also, explore WebMD's resourceful "Healthy Men" page at http://my.webmd.com to get answers to all your questions about your health.

- Ask a pharmacist or an AIDS Hotline counselor about an FDA-approved at-home HIV test kit, which allows you to test yourself for the virus and learn results in the privacy of your own home. Most pharmacies stock a variety of these kits.

- Share your newfound AIDS knowledge with your children, parents, friends, fellow church members and coworkers.

- Never let anyone force or convince you to do anything during sexual activity that makes you feel uncomfortable or could put you at risk.

- Today, buy and read the book *Sex: A Man's Guide*, by Stefan Bechtel, Laurence Roy Stains, and the editors of *Men's Health* books.

14. Remove the word *nigga* from your vocabulary.

A nickname is the heaviest stone the devil can throw at a man.

—Unknown

There's nothing more infuriating than to hear someone of a different race call a black person a "nigger." And growing up, many of us heard the word roll loosely off the tongues of the black adults we were supposed to respect and look up to. Were they respecting themselves and our people when they used this word? Certainly not.

One of the most infamous words in the English language, *nigger* has Latin roots in "niger," which evolved into "negro," and in the France of the Middle Ages, "negre." For the

French, Spanish, and Portuguese, these were not negative terms; they simply meant "black." It wasn't until the word made its way onto the scene during the era of slavery in the New World—as a corruption of the word *Negro*—that it possessed negative connotations. And the use of the word has remained a chief symbol of white racism and black self-hatred in America ever since.

Over the years in the black community, we have erroneously convinced ourselves that it's okay to "affectionately" call each other by the name, and its slightly altered derivative "*nigga*." We rationalize that we have taken the word that has demoted our being for hundreds of years, and empowered it with our own definitions. The word's popularity grows continuously in the rough rhymes of rap and other music, in which it is used synonymously with "homey," "my partner," "my ace," or to mean "I love you." However, unlike many other names by which we refer to each other in our community—"my boy," "boo," and "man," *nigga* is not a term of endearment.

Linguistic anthropologists say that disputes over the word often center around two factors: 1) who is saying it, and 2) a distinction some make between *nigga* and *nigger*. We all know that if a Caucasian person even fixes his or her mouth to say it, we're ready to "go Medieval" on 'em (even if he or she says it affectionately to "fit in"). Of course, in most cases, their use of the word does not have the same "loving" connotation that it supposedly does when folks of African descent say it.

Let's not uphold a double standard here. Have we become so far removed from our ancestors' struggle for respect in this world, that we fail to remember the evil American root of *nigger*? Let's not dis ourselves by continuing to validate the "N word." We deserve better.

Action Steps

- Encourage family members, friends, and colleagues—especially "old-school" adults and "Gen-Xers"—to discontinue their use of the word. Share with them the dangerous social consequences of using the evil nickname.

- Use respectful language when talking to or about others. You'll want the same respect.

- If you see the "N word" written as part of graffiti on a wall, erase it, or act to get it expunged. Leaving it there condones it.

15. Drink your liquor in moderation.

It is far easier to engage in too much or too little of
anything than to hit that special place called moderation.
—Johnnetta B. Cole, former president of Spelman College

Sister Cole is right. Listen up!

Social events often revolve around liquor. When we attend these gatherings, we are faced with deciding whether or not to indulge, and if we do, how much. Some of us like to partake of a spectrum of bottled spirits. Others decline. Whatever we choose, it is our personal decision, not the choice of those who coerce us to "go on and have (another) one."

An occasional drink or two is, for the most part, harmless, say many health officials. It is when we consume too much and too often that trouble sets in.

Remember, alcohol should never be what makes us sociable. If we enjoy its taste and the high it gives us, we must drink it responsibly and in moderation. So, next time you're "sipping" with the fellas, your partner, or kinfolk, monitor your intake; keep all your faculties in check. You should always be able to remember everything you did while drinking. Ask yourself if a night of getting "liquored up" is really worth embarrassing stories of your drunkenness or the dreaded "Alka-Seltzer moment" you'll have the next morning.

Responsible drinkers know their limits. Determine yours before someone else tells you.

Action Steps

- Never drink on an empty stomach. Before heading to the festivities, eat a little something or drink a glass of milk to coat the lining of your stomach, allowing alert thinking for a longer period of time.

- Never drink and drive. Even if you think you are okay, you run the risk of killing yourself or an innocent bystander. Stay put for a while following the after-dinner wine, or have a designated driver.

- Serve alcohol in your home responsibly. If you notice a guest is having one too many, cut off her/his drinks. By all means, don't let the person get behind the wheel to attempt to drive home. Slyly confiscate and hide her/his keys. Act like she or he misplaced the keys. You might suffer a little heat for doing so, but the person will live long enough to get over it.

- If you are a recovering alcoholic, steer clear of the booze and other drugs. When you find yourself feeling vulnerable to the bottle, get to the nearest Alcoholics Anonymous (AA) meeting or call your AA sponsor. Look up Alcoholics Anonymous in any telephone directory. In most urban areas, a central AA office, or "intergroup," staffed mainly by volunteers, will be happy to answer your questions or put you in touch with someone who can. You can write to: Alcoholics Anonymous World Services, Inc., P.O. Box 459, New York, NY 10163; the telephone number is: 212–870–3400.

- Learn more about Alcoholics Anonymous by visiting the Alcoholics Anonymous World Services, Inc. Web site at this address: http://www.alcoholics-anonymous.org/

■ Take this quiz, based on one developed by the National Institute on Alcohol Abuse and Alcoholism to identify problem drinkers:

Do you:

–think and talk about drinking often?

–drink more now than you used to?

–sometimes drink in gulps?

–frequently take a drink to relax?

–drink alone?

–sometimes forget what happened while you were "getting your sip on"?

–keep a bottle or flask hidden somewhere—at home, at the office, or in your car—for quick pick-me-ups?

–need to have a drink to loosen up enough to talk with others?

–just start drinking without even thinking about it?

–take a swig to take your mind off something that angers or has been bothering you?

–drink in the morning to relieve a hangover?

If you answered yes to any of the above questions, you may have a drinking problem and need to ask for and get help. Alcoholism affects men of all walks of life—rich, poor, or in-between; high IQ or average; confident or shy. Hiding or choosing to ignore your dependency on the bottle never helps; it always hurts in the long run.

16. Join a fraternal order or civic group.

You can't spell "brothers" without at the same time spelling "others."

—American proverb

Fraternities and certain civic groups have always provided a special place for men who want and need to enjoy "guy things." These types of groups also help bolster your network of professional friends, from those on college campuses to corporate boardrooms, and often offer support not found in traditional places.

Fraternities (especially African-American ones) provide a close-knit sense of bonding like no other found in human existence. There are often times that "brothers" in fraternities can share ideas, thoughts, and feelings with fellow "frats" that they cannot share with their family members.

Also, true "brothers" in fraternities or other fraternal organizations like the Masons, Shriners, or 100 Black Men of America will always be there to help you. There are limits, however. Quick joke: "If your brother has a car, you have a car; if your brother has a dollar, you have a dollar; if your brother has a babe, you still have a car and a dollar!"

Overall, most African-American member-based groups not only offer the personal, lifelong, lasting friendships that provide a pillar of assistance to individuals of like minds, they also provide service to those around them and those in need. In fact, a study at the University of Michigan found that men with weak social ties had higher death rates than those who were strongly connected to others. Just like playing on a softball team, getting together for a monthly game of poker, or participating in fellowship with others in church, being active in a fraternal order or civic group can offer a man a sense of belonging to a community. So, check 'em out.

Action Steps

- Talk with a buddy, relative, or business associate who is already involved in a fraternal order or civic group. Have him introduce you to some of the members to get their perspectives on the group.

- Review the tenets of different groups to see if they fit your interests, philosophies, and ideas.

- Be active with organizations that do important work in your community, even if you are not a member or don't wish to become one.

17. Get your groove on.

Go on wit'cha bad self, then!

—African-American saying

A man experiences many peaks and valleys during the course of his lifetime. Sometimes life's unpredictable rollercoaster ride can really throw him for a loop, leaving him feeling a little off kilter, somewhat blue, or even totally out of sync. Life-transitions, such as the adjustments to or ending of a marriage, the death of a loved one, or a midlife crisis are just a few of the happenings that can take the pep from our step, glide from our stride. It's in times like these a man's gotta do what a man's gotta do to feel better connected in life.

Getting your groove on is doing what makes you feel good inside, and every man gets his on in his own way. For you, maybe it's: Calling up one of the honeys whose seven digits you got at last night's cotillion. Gettin' your boogie on in just your socks and underwear to the soul-stirring sounds of Marvin Gaye, Prince, Destiny's Child, Outkast, or Tina Turner. Giving yourself a fresh new look with that haircut you've contemplated getting for weeks. Rewarding yourself with that hundred-dollar full-body massage from that cutie with da bomb body you met at the health club. Starting a new workout routine. Purchasing that three-button suit in the department-store window you've been eying for a month now. Learning that new dance that "everyone's doing" at all the parties these days. Sporting the black leather jacket you finally broke down and bought.

In essence, go on and do what makes you feel good inside, bruh. Give yourself that lift you need—and don't let anyone disturb your groove!

Action Steps

- Plan a vacation for one, which will give you the space and time you need to reflect on your life and set new goals.

- Go to church and connect yourself with the Spirit.

- Begin keeping a personal daily journal.

- Don't be afraid to dine out alone; realize that self can be the best company sometimes.

18. If you are age forty or older, have regular prostate exams.

Our habitual patterns and unresourceful behaviors exist only as long as we do nothing to change them. Recognize them, arrest them, interrupt them, and replace them, and life will change for the better.

—Joseph McClendon III, author

Prostate cancer kills an estimated 40,000 American men annually, and it is one of the toughest of all cancers to treat once it begins to spread. It is the second-leading cancer killer among American men overall—just after lung cancer. According to the National Cancer Institute, black men have the highest rate of prostate cancer worldwide. Prostate cancer occurs almost 70 percent more often in African-American men as it does in white American men. African-American men are twice as likely to die of prostate cancer as white men. According to the

American Cancer Society, it was projected that in 2001 alone, prostate cancer would be diagnosed in about 198,100 Americans and more than 31,500 men are expected to die of the disease. It is approaching lung cancer as the leading cause of cancer-related deaths in men of African descent.

Like high blood pressure, prostate cancer is also a "silent killer"—it usually lurks in a man's body without symptoms. Although the prostate gland may be low-key, when it acts up it doesn't half-step. So for you brothers who are over forty, this means you could be walking around feeling fine while the disease festers. It is not until the disease is well on its way that you notice something is wrong. Symptoms to look out for are hesitant or weak urine streams, a feeling of an unemptied bladder, and an increased need to "take a leak."

We are not doomed, however. There is something very basic you can do to help protect yourself and others from this dreadful disease: Go to the doctor's office for a complete physical each year. Along with the blood-pressure, cardiovascular, and diabetes exams, make sure your doctor conducts the infamous digital rectal exam (DRE), in which the doctor inserts a lubricated, gloved finger into the rectum to feel for hard or lumpy areas on the prostate. Many experts suggest that a DRE be performed in conjunction with a prostate-specific antigen (PSA) test. Unfortunately many of us fail to get this simple exam that can usually detect the cancer early enough to save our lives. Guys who remain in their "stubborn male" mode, not seeking proper preventative care, extend an open invitation to cancer. What's more is that the disease is more aggressive in young men in their late thirties and early forties.

Although the jury is still out on the accuracy of the PSA test, the American Cancer Society, the American Urological Society, and the American College of Radiology agree that routine screenings of most men should begin at age fifty.

However, African-American men or men with a history of prostate cancer in their families should begin getting screened at age forty.

Dying of prostate cancer does not have to be our fate. In fact, several black male celebrities and other public figures have faced the music, but danced to their own drums as prostate-cancer survivors—actors Sidney Poitier and Louis Gossett Jr.; former Washington, D.C., mayor Marion Barry; and singer-actor Harry Belafonte; former US ambassador and mayor of Atlanta Andrew Young, and motivational speaker Les Brown.

As we take responsibility for ourselves, let us encourage the other men in our lives—Pops, Uncle James, Granddaddy, and Reverend Smith—to heed this same warning. When the women in our lives push us to get checked out, let's do it not only for ourselves, but for them as well; they want us around for years to come.

While medical experts continue to search for answers, it is imperative that we keep abreast of the latest developments via the health-news media. We must also begin talking candidly with our doctors and with other men about the disease. We can no longer ignore the beast. Our keeping quiet could kill the rest of us.

Action Steps

- If you are age forty or over and have never had a digital rectal exam, make it a point to stop by your doctor's office this week to pick up a brochure on prostate cancer and make an appointment.

- Learn more about prostate cancer and other men's health issues by visiting the Black Health Network home page at http://www.blackhealthnetwork.com

- Practice good prostate self-care in the following ways:

–Empty your bladder before bedtime.

–Stay hydrated. Drink at least eight eight-ounce glasses of water a day. Reducing your fluid intake can predispose you to urinary infection.

–Take it easy on the spicy and acidic foods and drinks (e.g., hot sauce, jalapeño cornbread, citrus fruit juices, and soda pop).

–Keep your stress level down via regular exercise, deep-breathing techniques, meditation, or prayer, etc.

–See your doctor to rule out other health problems.

- If you are living with prostate cancer, follow your doctor's orders to the letter. They're for your own good.

- Don't be embarrassed to discuss your prostate condition with those who love and care about you. They will support you and will be there when you just need to talk.

- Before you undergo a PSA test, know the risks and benefits. Understand how to interpret your PSA test. Ask the doctor to break down the results in "layman's terms" for you. You should not leave the office with questions.

- Know that getting a digital rectal exam will not challenge your manhood. It's your health we're talking about, brother!

- If cancer is found to be present after your PSA test, ask your doctor whether or not it is confined to your prostate.

- Don't be shy about telling your doctor you want a second opinion. It's *your* body.

- If the doctor says you need surgery, make sure the surgeon who conducts the procedure comes highly recommended.

- Know the Seven Warning Signs of Cancer:

  Change in bowel or bladder habits
  A sore throat that doesn't heal
  Unusual bleeding or discharge

Thickening or lump in the breast or elsewhere
Indigestion or difficulty in swallowing
Obvious change in a wart or mole
Nagging cough or hoarseness

19. Read. Read. Read.

*If I was not reading in the [prison] library, I was reading on
my bunk. You couldn't have gotten me out of a book with
a wedge.*

—Malcolm X, civil-rights leader

Nothing liberates a man's mind like reading. He who has the
good fortune of knowing how to read must treasure this invaluable skill. When we gather information from books,
newspapers, and magazines, we open new worlds for ourselves.

As enslaved people of color struggling to speak the foreign
English tongue, we were legally denied the opportunity to
read and write. Keeping us gullible and ignorant was the
slaveowners' way of keeping us from "gettin' any ideas."
Still, our shackled brothers and sisters secretly quenched
their thirst for knowledge by teaching themselves to read and
write by candlelight in the confines of their cabins. They
pressed on to feed and free their minds, even though they
were aware that if caught, they could suffer violent consequences. In their quest, they were paving a brighter and more
prosperous future for themselves and their descendants.

When our children witness our love for books, it sends an
encouraging message to them that says reading is not only
fundamental, it's rewarding and even fun!

Today in America, when freedom has never been greater,
each of us should read with the same desire and spirited

efforts our ancestors did. Let us have a hearty appetite for reading everything we can get our hands on. Being a well-read person enables us to better articulate and express ourselves in writing and speaking. Increasing our reading time stimulates the mind, keeps it young. Relying too heavily upon the convenience of television newscasts, talk shows, and serials to give us information, we limit ourselves to digesting biased viewpoints. Instead we must invest more of our time in reading the printed word, interpreting for ourselves the meaning of ideas and messages being presented.

Dive into a good read today. The knowledge awaits you!

Action Steps

- Read everything you can get your hands on. A well-read brother should be familiar with:

    –books—from classic literature and world history to children's stories and current events

    –newspapers—from local community newspapers to major dailies like *USA Today* and *The Wall Street Journal*

    –magazines—from popular periodicals like *Savoy* and *Men's Health* to major news weeklies like *Time* and *Newsweek*

- If you (or someone you know) cannot read very well and need(s) a booster, rather than feeling ashamed or embarrassed, do something about it today. You can always contact your local school system or the public library for assistance.

- Teach an elderly or young person how to read. You will open a whole new world for him or her. Senior-citizen centers and educational institutions are always looking for volunteer tutors.

- While reading, when you come across words you do not know, stop to jot them down and look them up in the dictionary to find out what they mean. You will increase your vocabulary, and doing so helps you to better understand what you read.

- Read everything requiring your signature carefully before you sign it—especially the fine print.
- Join a local book club in which members pick, read, and discuss a book of the month. Or better yet, start your own brothers book club!
- Spread the written word—give books at Christmastime, Kwanzaa, and on birthdays.

20. Don't make a baby you're not ready to father.

When I have a kid, I want to be into the kid. I want to go into fatherhood the same way I go into work—I want to give it my all.

—Chris Rock, entertainer

It's been said that most any male can make a baby, but it takes a real man to father one. It takes a wise man to know the difference.

In recent years, the number of African-American men producing babies out of wedlock has soared to an unimaginable level. Many of these men have simply become baby-making machines—some without knowledge of the life they have created. Protecting themselves and their partners from pregnancy or sexually transmitted diseases is the last thing on their minds while in the "heat of the moment." Their goal is to simply "hit it and quit it" with the women whom they bed (or the women who bed them).

As stated earlier, according to the Urban Institute in Washington, young black males between the ages of fifteen and twenty-four are out there having sex like there is no tomorrow—and at the rate they are spreading AIDS, there may well not be one. This group is the least likely of any to use a condom. Sisters represent the fastest growing group with AIDS, and they still won't insist that brothers use a condom.

What's even more disturbing is that many of the women with whom these men "get their swerve on" actually want a baby—with no strings attached, not even as much as a commitment from their partners to provide for or support the baby. This is not in any way to suggest that there is anything wrong or shameful about single parenthood. What is wrong is when neither the woman nor the man is able to provide for the baby with not only love, but also the adequate financial support and emotional stability needed early on for the child to live a healthy and productive life as an adult.

C'mon, fellas. Actually making a baby requires little beyond fifteen minutes of meaningless bumping, grinding, coming and waiting to see what happens. Not much to it, right? No emotional attachment required. Simple as that. However, consciously fathering a child means to be passionately connected to your mate, who shares your desire to produce a little one. This baby will need to depend on an attentive, responsible mother and father to provide and care for it.

Remember, men, to be a true father is to do the 3 A.M. feedings. To change the stinky diapers. To witness the first step. To bandage a scraped knee. To instruct the first bicycle ride without training wheels. To be there for that first Little League game. To answer the first sex question. To make every PTA meeting at school. Get the point? If you and your partner insist on "doin' the wild thing" without protecting yourselves, make sure you're ready for the potential consequences to follow. Yours, your partner's, and an innocent baby's health and life could be at stake.

Action Steps

- If you're sexually active and don't wish to be a father or don't want to contract a sexually transmitted disease, make sure you and your partner are properly protected, using products and methods that are as foolproof as possible.
- Before you "do it," make sure you're ready. Don't be pressured by anyone.
- Be cautious of the woman who tells you she wants you to be "just her baby's daddy."
- If you or your mate is considering single parenthood, weigh all the options. Think about how it will affect the two of you, and how it will affect your offspring.

21. Be happy.

"Don't worry. Be happy."

—Bobby McFerrin, entertainer

Brother Bobby told us this years ago. If it were only that simple, some thought. Well, guess what. It *is* that simple. You determine whether or not happiness is incorporated into your life.

Many of us rarely take the time to give thought to what truly makes us happy. That may be one of the very reasons we have so many worries. Ask yourself what really makes you happy. Spending time with your wife? Watching your daughter ice skate? Cruising in your new sports car? Seeing your favorite team score a touchdown? Sunday-morning service? Think. What really makes you "cheese" ear to ear?

In life there are many ups and downs; that's part of the deal we got when we emerged from the womb. Yet, while disappointments drag us down, we have the power to pick ourselves up, brush ourselves off, and start again.

Every man should be able to leave this world feeling as though he led a happy and productive life. However, to be happy, we must first determine what makes us that way, then live and experience in that way.

Money may help, but it is not the total answer. It may bring you comfort and convenience and sometimes even power, but money never buys happiness. So, be careful not to equate money with happiness, for you'll surely be disappointed.

Remember, the simple things in life bring happiness. Those things that money can't buy—like good health, spirituality, the love of family and friends and our significant others.

Action Steps

- Laugh. It's good for you. Learn to laugh at yourself, not just at or with others.
- Relax whenever you can. Tense feelings and moods can be soothed by sitting back and just "chillin' out." Before the end of today, get somewhere alone, and spend ten or fifteen minutes with your eyes closed; lie on your back and recall something that warmed your heart and brought a smile to your face.
- Let go of old baggage—it does nothing but hold you back.
- Live without regret.
- Live in the moment. Tomorrow is not promised.

22. Support black businesses.

My father was the kind who would say, "If a black man opens a store, go shop in it."

—Rev. Calvin O. Butts III, pastor of the historic
Abyssinian Baptist Church of New York

In some communities, a dollar changes hands seven times among various members of the community before it is spent outside of that community. This is not so for the African-American community.

It is vital for the survival of the African-American community that we spend our dollars where we live and work. This is not segregation; this is an age-old tradition of building a village that is self-sufficient by reinvesting in your neighborhoods and communities so they flourish instead of border on extinction.

Auburn Avenue in Atlanta, Georgia, is a prime example. It was dubbed the "black Wall Street" of America in the mid-twentieth century. It has since lost its luster. No longer is "Sweet Auburn" as enterprising as it once was. Now, instead of booming businesses, there are many empty buildings and vacant lots. Many African Americans have abandoned it, only to patronize suburban shopping malls located nowhere near black neighborhoods. Thus, the dollar that, at one time, was exchanged by several black hands now goes directly to other communities as fast as we can cash our paychecks—and even faster if we're not depositing our money into African-American–owned banks.

We must patronize black businesses even if it means driving a few extra miles or mail-ordering to do it. Let's face it, the small black-owned business does not have a franchise on every corner. The extra trip we make to patronize it can help make the owner's dream of expansion become reality.

We also can help African-American businesses do better by not dismissing them if their service isn't up to par. When the quality of service doesn't meet our expectations, we have to speak up, letting the manager or owner know of our displeasure. Everyone deserves a second chance. Then, if after the second go-around we're still not satisfied, we should seek out another African-American business that does meet our consumer expectations. However, as a parting tip, let the business know why you are leaving, and what it would take to get you back.

The Million Man March included a defining moment that perfectly symbolized the power of black economic unity. Asked by one of the speakers to make personal contributions, a million-plus black hands shot up into the air, each clutching a one-dollar bill. The free giving of those dollars exemplified one of the seven principals of Kwanzaa: *Ujamaa,* which means "cooperative economics." Let us live in the spirit of Ujamaa so we may profit collectively as a people.

Action Steps

- If you don't already have one, open a checking or a savings account at a black-owned bank.
- Shop in black neighborhoods.
- Challenge your friends and relatives to invest dollars back in our community by making referrals. Word of mouth can make or break a business.
- Launch an organized effort to get civic and business leaders to develop business in the black community. Use your buying clout as leverage.

23. Don't dictate your life around what other people think.

I don't know the key to success, but the key to failure is to try to please everyone.

—Bill Cosby, entertainer

Since the day we learned we must please other people, we have been doing just that—sometimes to our detriment. We seek to please folks at work. We seek to please them at home.

We seek to please them on the football field. We seek to please them even in our places of worship.

Others may want us to do what they say, whether it's to adopt a particular religious belief, to raise our children in a certain way, or to follow a certain lifestyle. They may not understand the choices we make for ourselves and our loved ones. They may call you crazy. Scrutinize you. Condemn you. Make you feel guilty. They may even try to strong-arm you into doing things their way.

Obviously, there are some arrangements under which we must answer to others, like on the job, in the classroom, or under "Mama's roof," etc. However, we must first be accountable to ourselves. Although we might listen and even consider the views of others, only *we* know a good fit for ourselves when we feel one.

On the journey of life, we make many choices for ourselves that affect the routes we take. Sometimes we make bad choices. Sometimes we make good ones. What we must bear in mind, however, is that it is *our* life and *we* have to live it.

So, next time your critics and naysayers doubt and condemn you, hold your ground. Hang tough. Pray for strength, courage and wisdom if you must. And what if they later prove you wrong? Just remember, personal mistakes are ones you also can call your own. Expect to make them, learn from them, and move on.

Action Steps

- Be open to others' ideas and suggestions. Sometimes you need a perspective other than your own.

- Don't waste time or energy responding to your critics—they're not obliged to prove a thing.

- Remember, what other people say about you is none of your business.

- Ask yourself: "Am I driving my life, or is someone else?"

- Unburden yourself of the "disease to please." It'll change your life!

24. Reconnect with your dad.

The best way to end a war is not to begin it.

—Unknown

A man's early relationship with his father follows him through his adulthood, affecting his self-esteem, self-confidence, and quality of his romantic relationships. Yet many a brother is emotionally estranged from his father, with negative results.

Men who are merely estranged from their fathers should count their blessings; they're lucky to still have him among the living. A "disconnect" can be repaired. However, for others who don't know their dad, or whose father is deceased—that can leave a hole in the soul. Of course, some father-son relationships are irreconcilable; this is a reality, a part of life. Yet for those fathers and sons who have a disconnect for silly or foolish reasons—a falling out over petty money matters, Dad's new wife, or inherited material property—both men should think about what they're missing and how much time is being wasted. Our stay here on earth is too short for life-long disconnects.

As men, we have a strong tendency to let stubborn pride get in the way of how we may really be feeling. We continue to stay mute, never telling a parent how we feel or acting to rekindle what has the potential to be a very fruitful relationship. Holding on to old grudges and harboring resentment only worsens old wounds, broken hearts, and big disappointments. We only have one father (or father figure), and if circumstances are right, those who are estranged must find ways to bridge the distance. It doesn't matter who was right or who was wrong. Anger, blame, and finger-pointing has no home here. Rather, as you work to reconnect, approach your father with compassion. Begin with an open mind, a calm head, forgiving heart, and a willingness to not just hear the other side's point of view, but to listen, really listen. It will take time. It will take patience. However, with strong determination and loving hearts, both you and your dad can begin bridging the gap and building a healthy father-son relationship.

There are many ways you can begin reconnecting with your dad today. Below are just a few ideas to get you started forging the links:

Action Steps

- Gradually begin calling or dropping by to see him once or twice a week just to say, "Hey, Pop. How ya doin'?"
- Get to know the man behind your dad. Ask him about his life as a young man, or how he met your mother.
- Find out how your dad is doing by asking other family members. Let them know it's okay for them to let him know you've been asking about him.
- Have your "old man" over for a dinner of his favorite foods.
- Make the contact personal by writing him a note, recalling a memorable time that you and he had together when you were a child. Maybe include a line about how, as you grow older, you're beginning to see his positive traits or physical characteristics in yourself.
- Send him a few photographs of your children if you are a dad, too. More than likely his eyes will light up when he sees how fine his grandchildren have grown up so quickly.
- Ask him about his health. Let him know you're concerned about his welfare. Then tell him how *your* health is.

- To help enhance the reconnection, suggest that the two of you take a class together, like computers, drawing, or automotive or home repair (since hobby workshops are nonthreatening), to get you talking.

- Don't forget to tell him how much you've missed his presence in your life. Then uncross your arms and hold him tight.

25. Be able to sleep at night.

This is my last interview. If I get killed, I want people to get every drop. I want them to have my real story.
                                    —Tupac Shakur, entertainer

The story of rapper Tupac Shakur being the target of gunfire twice over and then ultimately dying as a result is a good example—albeit an extreme one—of a brother who probably wasn't able to sleep at night.

After watching the Mike Tyson–Bruce Seldon fight on September 7, 1996, Shakur, age twenty-five, didn't survive the last episode of facing the barrel of a gun. He died several days later from his wounds. It was the second time he had been gunned down in less than two years. In November 1994, he was shot five times during an apparent robbery in the lobby of a Manhattan recording studio.

In the late rapper's song "Life Goes On," Tupac raps about his own funeral. Just a few days after his death, his music video "I Ain't Mad At Cha'" was released. The video shows Tupac as an angel in heaven. In the video, Tupac was shot after leaving a theater. He was also up-front about his troubled life in the 1995 release of *Me Against the World*, a multi-million-selling CD that contained the ominously titled tracks, "If I Die 2Nite" and "Death Around the Corner." Eerily, sources close to the slain rapper say Tupac was a restless soul, often predicting his own death through the lyrics of his tunes and in videos that depicted his own mortality. Others who had met him, had business dealings with him, or interviewed him have often recalled his references to whether or not he'd see past the present day.

Having led life in the fast lane of close calls and pandemonium, it's hard to imagine how in the world this brother slept at night. From the outside looking in, it had to be difficult.

Of course, the lives of most men who lie awake at night hardly come close to resembling what appeared to be the horrific life of Tupac. However, our own woes can keep us up at night, pondering how to get through it all. A drawerful of delinquent bills and maxed-out credit cards. An ongoing battle with the bottle. Waiting for the lie we told the boss to blow up in our face. The woman who's threatening to expose your affair.

Whether or not you are a fan or endorse the choices he made, Tupac Shakur was one of the most successful "gangsta" rappers of our time. Fans bought millions of his records. Others denounced him and his lyrics for glorifying violence and drugs and degrading women. Ultimately, he was another young brother to add to the ever-expanding black-male homicide file.

Tomorrow is not promised even when we're living life on the right side of the tracks. Therefore, let us not flirt with danger or teeter on the brink of destruction. Life is too precious. Let us, when we turn out our lights at night, know we've lived a righteous life. A peaceful life. A hazard-free life. A damn good life. Sleep tight, brother. You won't rest until you do.

Action Steps

- Choose your companions carefully.
- Live within your budget.

- Depressed? Angry? Addicted? Anxious? Begin dealing with your problems now.
- Be honest with yourself and others.
- Seek the guidance you need through prayer and/or meditation.
- Pay off your debts in a timely manner.
- This week, resolve an issue with which you have been struggling.
- Forgive yourself for something you did ages ago. Letting go of the guilt is paramount for healing old wounds.
- Apologize to someone you have angered or hurt with your clenched fists, swift kick, or hateful words.
- Confront the something or the someone haunting you.
- If you feel you can't lay an issue to rest, seek professional help. Counselors and advisers are available to listen most anywhere—on the campus, in a house of worship, and through work-related employee assistance programs (EAPs), just to name a few.

26. Have a vision.

I have the original vision, and I see the film in its finished form before one frame is shot. When you get people dickering with your stuff, it distorts the vision.

—Spike Lee, filmmaker and entertainer

We hear it all the time: "If you can see it, you can achieve it." As clichéd as it sounds, the old saying makes a whole lot of sense. It's been proven to work time and time again. Just ask someone who's made his or her visions into realities.

Visualization is nothing more than seeing what we want to happen before it actually does. It's using your imagination to create scenes of the things we desire in our hearts. When setting goals, making new year's resolutions, or making life-changing choices, we must envision ourselves smack-dab in the middle of the situation to which we aspire.

Want that new sport utility vehicle? Picture yourself driving toward the horizon in the driver's seat of a new Ford Explorer or Lincoln Navigator. Take a deep breath and smell its newness. Feel the comfortable leather seats. Want the promotion at the office? Imagine yourself proudly giving your first new business card bearing your new job title to one of your clients. In your mind, materialize a vivid color photo in the employee newsletter. Want the beautiful wife, home, kids, and family dog? Envision yourself and your loved ones walking through the front door for the first time. In your mind, walk through each fully furnished room with smiles on your faces. See yourselves giving thanks at the dining-room table covered with a soul-food feast. Feel the moment. Smell it. Taste it. Reflect on it. Get the picture?

When we can capture in our minds the things we want for ourselves, we provide our spirit with not only the encouragement it needs, but the reinforcement it requires during the journey. The mind is a unique and powerful tool we've been given, and we can use it effectively to make our wants and wishes realities. We are limited only by our own imagination.

Action Steps

- When trying the above exercises, don't be discouraged if the images don't materialize immediately. Have patience and be persistent. Practice daily. (And don't try this exercise while driving.)

- Buy an 18-x-12-inch sketch pad and fill the blank white pages with images of things you'd like to own—a particular style of house, power drill, computer desk, drafting table, boat, piece of exercise equipment for your workout room at home. Cut out images from old magazines, newspapers, and the like. Put a photo of yourself in the middle of the page, surrounding it with those images. This will allow you to keep a visual record of the things you want.

- Pray sensibly for your heart's desires.

- Share your vision with your mate, your best friend, or parents.

- Pick up a copy of the book *The Prayer of Jabez,* by Bruce H. Wilkinson. Its message will compliment your vision exercise and change the way you pray.

27. Practice good personal hygiene.

Sooner or later, we've got to polish ourselves up; we've got to let the shine through.
—Lou Rawls, entertainer

Most of us know someone who has poor personal hygiene. It's all we can do to not offer him a breath mint, soap and a washcloth, deodorant, or a comb. The stench can turn our stomach, and we nearly suffocate as we look for a quick escape from the room.

That is why we must check *ourselves* before we criticize others. We may think we have it goin' on, but sometimes it's the little things we forget to do.

It used to be that for men, as long as we lathered up with soap-on-a-rope, brushed the teeth, deodorized our armpits every day, and got a haircut every now and then, we were doing enough. Think again. The well-groomed man takes care of his body and makes sure he's fit for public appearance at all times. Even "tough" guys like NFL running back Craig "Ironhead" Heyward boasts of the benefits of using a refreshing body wash and his body pouf. So, even the burliest of men realize the importance of self body-care.

However, to be well groomed, we shouldn't have to completely rearrange our lives. Just adding a few minor but necessary rituals to our self-care and -pampering routines can leave us feeling fresh and looking great.

Action Steps

- Schedule an appointment to get a professional manicure. As with regular haircuts, "real" men of the new millennium get regular manicures to ensure healthy fingernails, cuticles, and good-looking hands. They're inexpensive, and many barbershops now have licensed manicurists and pedicurists set up on site; make sure your nail-care professional is reputable and always uses sterile tools.

- Schedule an appointment for a professional pedicure. Like manicures, they never have been just for women. Many men are finally waking up to the fact that neglecting our feet doesn't equate with being a man—it simply means we're abusing our feet. Remember, layered, cracked, jagged, yellowed, or blackened toenails; overgrown cuticles; "jacked-up" toes and crusty heels, corns, and calluses are unhealthy—not to mention repulsive. In some cases (e.g., black or green toenails), medical care by a podiatrist may be necessary for curing. Pull off the socks now and take a good look at your bare feet. Do they need attention? If so, stop neglecting your potentially fungus-laden feet, and call for that appointment today!

- Keep your fingernails and toenails clipped, filed, and clean in between visits.

- When working out, wear fresh, absorbent athletic socks, preferably with a polypropylene lining, to absorb perspiration from the skin. One pair of cotton socks won't do it if your feet tend to smell.

- Check your nose and ears for wild hairs. Yep, those little hairs that tickle the old sniffer, making you dig, scratch, and wiggle. The moment you see them, clip them. They make you appear unkempt.

- Take a bath instead of a shower sometimes. In today's fast-paced world, you barely have time to take a long shower, let alone take a bath. You need to make the time, at least a couple of times a week, to bathe. Baths have never been just for women, children, and dogs. That soaking time is ideal for unwinding after a long day on the job, on the campus, or after your workout at the gym. A bath can soothe the overworked mind and body, loosen dirt in the skin that a shower won't, and relax tight muscles from neck to toe. Besides, why should women, children, and dogs be any cleaner than we are?

- Sprinkle baby or foot powder inside your shoes and in between your toes after bathing or showering for a soothing sensation.

- Moisturize your body. Let's face it, fellas. Ashy feet, legs, and elbows are a turn-off in socks, in pants, in shirts, and in bed. They simply don't feel good. Many of us hop right out of the shower or finish washing up without putting a lick of lotion on our skin, but we don't go a day without greasing or moisturizing our hair. With the right moisturizing soap and lotion, your skin can be as soft as your mane. After bathing or showering, it's essential to use a thick, absorbent towel to dry off, leaving the skin slightly moist. Apply the moisturizer or lotion to your damp skin, locking in just the right amount of moisture.

- Sniff yourself. If you've had a long day and it ain't over yet, in private, take a quick whiff of the old armpits to make sure your antiperspirant/deodorant hasn't failed you. Keep a spare antiperspirant/deodorant stick at the office.

- Check your breath. If you are going to be in the company of others, do a quick hand-to-mouth breath-check to ensure your breath is not "wolfin'." Check yourself throughout the day. It's also a good idea to keep breath mints or spray in your pocket or briefcase.

- Make sure your barber disinfects the clippers, combs, and other tools just before using them on your hair. In addition to soaking them in that tall container of a blue disinfecting solution, he or she should also be washing them with good old-fashioned hot, soapy water. If you are not sure you're truly getting a "clean cut," on your next visit, candidly ask your barber if the tools have been thoroughly washed and disinfected since being used on the head before yours. As a paying client, you have the right to a healthy haircut.

- Check your fragrance-bottle "gauge." If people can smell you coming and going, you're wearing too much. Aftershaves, colognes, and body sprays should be worn conservatively. It's a personal thing, that scent is. Choose your fragrances wisely. Try to select scents that everyone else isn't wearing.

- Bottom line: Ignore your teeth and they will go away. You should brush and floss at least twice a day—morning and at bedtime. Healthy teeth and gums look good and can last a lifetime, and that's what you should be striving for when it comes to dental care. Getting regular dental checkups (every six months) is a must. Doing so prevents not only cavities, but also periodontal disease, bad breath, and unnecessary tooth loss. Proper maintenance will also save you lots of money. Don't be a "yuck mouth."

- Trim your hairline. Admit it, we have all seen it on others (if not on ourselves): hair growing like wild ivy on the back of the neck. It looks bad, bro. So, don't mirror that image. Look at the hairline on the back of your neck. Sometimes simple self-trimming of your hairline can give the appearance of a fresh haircut. So, in between barber visits, keep this hairline well groomed with a hair-trimmer.

- Keep a close eye on the back base of your neck. See any yellow or red bumps? If so, you may have pseudofolliculitis, a

condition to which black men are very susceptible, particularly those with curly hair. Do something to heal them
quickly. Ask your doctor for advice on home treatment. However, if you have a lingering condition, see a dermatologist.
Remember, too, don't pop or pick them; their bacterial secre-
tions may make them multiply on the rest of your scalp and
skin.

- Always wear thongs (flips-flops), or shower shoes while
  using communal showers (e.g., at the gym, health club,
  or public pool). If you don't, you stand a pretty good
  chance of catching the dreaded foot fungus called athlete's
  foot.

- Keep your hair "down there" well-groomed. Matted,
  knotted-up, dry, overgrown hair looks nasty, not manly, bro.
  Make combing, brushing, and moisturizing body hair part of
  your daily hygienic routine—and don't forget to keep it
  neatly trimmed.

- Wash those hands after using the john. Recent studies have
  shown men are more likely than women to skip the sink.
  Taking "a dump" or "a leak" without washing up afterward
  increases your chances of contracting bacteria-borne illnesses,
  from the common cold to diarrhea. While we may think we
  don't have to hand-wash after a pee, because we have
  touched nothing but our own skin, we may fail to realize that
  that penis skin is loaded with bacteria. So, always wash
  hands, wrists, and under the nails with warm or hot, soapy
  water, rubbing hands together for at least fifteen seconds.
  Then rinse, dry, and be on your way. Remember to use something other than your bare hand to pull open the door on
  your way out; a paper towel or the back of your tie are smart
  picks. Keep in mind, many of the guys who left before you
  didn't wash, and their germy residue awaits you!

- Carry pocket-size antibacterial hand-sanitizers and lotions in
  your attaché case or pocket. They're great substitutes when
  soap and water aren't available.

- Avoid jock itch. It can be your worst nightmare. It thrives in hot, moist areas of the groin. The chafing caused by clothing makes the problem worse. Symptoms include itching of your "private parts," accompanied by redness, oozing, and scaling in your groin area. There are a number of antiperspirant and antiyeast sprays and powders formulated to treat the problem. You can avoid getting jock itch by keeping pubic hair well-groomed, changing your underwear daily, and washing dirty clothes before fungus sets in. Don't let your workout clothes sit in the hamper for weeks on end. Finally, by no means should you work out and then put your gym wear back in your locker for tomorrow's workout!

- Follow the lead of some of your favorite NBA and NFL players who know what to do to look their best: get routine facials. A facial is designed to deep-cleanse, tone, and moisturize the skin. There are many different kinds of facials, and any reputable unisex day spa can hook you up with the one that best suits your skin type to keep your "mug" looking fresh!

28. Save. Save. Save.

Save money, and money will save you.

—Jamaican proverb

Living every day like it's your last is fine. However, if tomorrow shows up and you have nothing saved to enjoy that day, life will be pretty dismal. So it is vital to plan for tomorrow by saving today.

You know how your grandmother always had cash—in her Bible, under her mattress, and in her bosom? Well, Grandmother was a wise woman—she kept money in several places. Of course times have changed; now the Good Book can be an IRA, the mattress can be a special savings account, and the bosom can be money you send home to Mama to tuck away as your "rainy day" fund. Whatever you do, find a way to put a little away each pay period. You'll be surprised how it all adds up from year to year. A dollar a day will save you $365 a year. With savings accounts, the money you're depositing will draw interest over time—thus your money begins to work for you instead of you working for your money.

So, save, save, save. Then save some more. That way, you'll always have "rainy-day" money just like Grandmother.

Action Steps

- Stop nickle-and-diming your bank account by making multiple visits to the ATM—you will quickly rob yourself. Take out what you need once a week (perhaps on payday). So, when it's gone, it's gone.

- Invest in a good savings plan: IRAs, CDs, or a 401(k) plan at work. You may want to attend a financial-planning seminar or seek advice from a financial adviser.

- Hire an accountant (if you can afford one) to help file your taxes; he or she can help you save money when paying Uncle Sam—dollars you should invest, not spend.

- Be financially smart. Learn everything you can about investing, the stock market, and other financial matters. You can take a course or get free assistance where it's available.

- Never measure your riches in dollars alone.

- Know the current value of your 401(k) investment.

- Buy a book on basic personal financing.

- Remember: Money can't buy you happiness, but it sure can buy lots of perfectly nice substitutes!

29. Make peace with the size of your penis.

Size and shape myths, appetite and performance myths, clock and calendar myths, what works and what doesn't myths; it's an endless medley of fiction and fable that can cause you to look disapprovingly at your mate—and yourself. Great sex is nearly impossible under these influences.

—Dr. Ronn Elmore, author, psychotherapist, and minister

Truth be told, we fellas have been obsessing about the size of our members for centuries. The bigger the better, we think. Unfortunately, men—especially brothers—have been conditioned to think we are inferior if we're not as well endowed as the next guy. All you have to do is look at the way black men have been illustrated in books, on television, and in movies, and you get a sense of the characterization. We are often called "Mandingo," "Long John," and depicted as sex-driven black bucks.

Many of us feel we have to live up to "the myth." We don't. All men are not created equal when it comes to our anatomy. That's not a bad thing, brother. One brother's five inches may be a blessing, while another brother's eight may lead to his occasional inability to get an erection or can limit his depth of thrust. Some of us point north, some of us curve to the east or west. In fact, several sex surveys have revealed that many women don't prefer the "monstrous" member many guys secretly wish they had. While extra inches may be intriguing at a glance, said those surveyed, they can be uncomfortable and sometimes even inhibiting. So, bigger is not always better.

Remember, it's not how good it looks but how well it functions. Let's stop comparing, wishing, and hoping for something we really don't need. Even if you think you are too small, you're probably closer to average than you think. You are equipped with everything you need to satisfy during both partner and solo sex. Relax, be confident—not cocky—and accept yourself just the way you are.

So, how big should a penis be? Small enough to fit through the doorway and large enough to find in the dark.

Action Steps

- Affirm to yourself that you "measure up" just the way you are. Know you are structured just right for enjoying the most passionate and exciting experiences with your partner.

- Know that "The Myth" about black men is just that—a myth. Just like men of other colors and ethnic backgrounds, we, too, come in many different shades, shapes, and sizes. That's one of the things that makes us intriguing and worth the wait!

30. Find a faith and live by it.

[O]ur Creator is the same and never changes despite the name given Him by the people here and in all parts of the world.

—George Washington Carver, agricultural scientist

On the whole, African Americans are very spiritual people. We've had to be. Our strong faith in a higher power has kept us afloat since our turbulent journey by ship from the Motherland. Our rough ride continues with the unique challenges we face today. However, our light of hope for a better tomorrow burns much brighter when we have something to believe in, something to grasp.

Many of us are most familiar with the religions under which our families reared us. But how many of us have taken the time to fully understand them? On what are our religious faiths based? Are they the right ones for us? We must dig deep to truly understand our religions and what they are based upon. Should we discover that the one we're practicing is not appropriate for us, we must seek to explore and understand others that may better suit us individually.

God can come in many forms. And remember, God would not have created such a diverse worldwide population of people and only one designated way for us to serve.

As responsible brothers, we must explore and query the philosophy of religions other than our own. It is possible that after careful consideration and enlightenment, it could be that we have blindly followed a religious pattern that is inconsistent with our personal beliefs, values, and understanding of the higher power that guides us. Our families may shun us and our church leaders may wince. No matter—for we must each feel comfortable with the faith by which we practice and live.

It is said that men who live by strong faith have been known to live longer and more abundant lives. That's good news for brothers! A study of black men, conducted in 1994 by Wayne State University in Detroit, Michigan, showed a positive correlation between their health status and their denominational affiliation, frequency of church attendance, and overall spirituality. The report revealed that men who were regular churchgoers were less depressed and overall led healthier lives.

When we have a strong faith to walk by, we are equipped with a personal guide to lead us on the journey of life, a personal code to live by. Finding the right spiritual fit for ourselves as individuals can bring us all the blessings, joy and abundance we can stand!

Action Steps

- If you have no faith, examine several before deciding which one to follow.
- Find a place of worship in which you feel "at home," and attend services regularly.
- Get to know the leaders of your place of worship, and make sure they know you by name.
- Make time to pray not only for, but *with*, the people you love.
- Don't be embarrassed to pray in the presence of others (e.g., during lunch with coworkers, over dinner with clients, or during the last quarter of the big game).
- Respect others' religions as you would want them to respect yours.
- Pray for the black race. Given our global state, we need continuous blessings, guidance, and strength.
- Participate in the activities of your place of worship; they exist seven days a week, not just on Sunday.
- Have a moment of prayer or meditation when you wake and before you go to sleep.

31. Keep up with current events.

Ignorance doesn't kill you, but it makes you sweat a lot.

—Haitian proverb

Information is power.

If you plan to be one of the powerful, you need to stay abreast of what's going on. No, not just what's going on in the 'hood,' but what's happening in your city, your state, your country, and yes, your world.

An event in a country halfway around the globe can have a profound effect on you. It could be a good one, like an opportunity for you to invest in the new South Africa. Or it could be a negative, like an armed conflict in the Middle East, which could result in higher gasoline prices in the United States.

All too often, some men in the black community are not up on the important things that can have great impact on our daily lives. We may be enlightened about who won the football game Monday night, or which team the Lakers beat on the basketball court, or how many home runs Barry Bonds had, but do we know what issues are coming before brother Clarence Thomas and the other justices on the Supreme Court? Do we know the presidential administration's stance on stem-cell research and human cloning? Do we know who sits on the school board that oversees the schools our children attend? Do we know who our representative in Congress is and what he or she stands for?

The key, guys, is knowledge and knowing how to use it. When it comes to current events, it's not a bad idea to be an inch thick and a mile wide. Knowing a little bit about a lot of things arms you with the ability to hold intelligent conversations on a variety of subjects. Of course, delve into the things that interest you with even greater attention.

The way to obtain all this information is to read newspapers, watch or listen to the news. Don't just settle for local news. Watch the *News Hour with Jim Leher* and watch major network news programs. You can even listen to talk radio to pick up on what's going on here in the United States and overseas.

The more you read, the more you know. The more you know, the more you grow.

Action Steps

- Start reading the daily newspaper.

- Listen to National Public Radio on the way to work or during the drive home. You will have the world brought right into your car or your headset on the bus or train.

- Make sure you attend a city council or county commission meeting at least four times a year. Knowing your local representatives by sight will help you stay abreast of what's happening and how it could affect you and your family.
- Call or write your congressman, and find out what's going on.
- Meet with your neighborhood block or community club.
- Start a dialogue with the local beat cop in your neighborhood.
- Talk to students in college and high school about what current events are discussed in classes. Students often are more informed than adults who aren't taking any classes.

32. Understand what it *really* means to be a man.

The ultimate measure of a man is not where he stands in moments of comfort and convenience, but where he stands at times of challenge and controversy.
—Rev. Dr. Martin Luther King Jr., civil-rights leader

Many of us are so obsessed with being "man enough," we can't see the forest for the trees. We let television, movies, and other media define manhood for us. We let peers dictate and shape our opinions of what being a man is all about. When all is said and done, though, a man is one who measures up when it comes to the basics, like being responsible for his actions, caring for his family, keeping his word, respecting himself, and respecting others.

A real man loves and honors his mother and father. A real man loves, teaches, and learns from his children. A real man helps keep the house in order. A real man does not waste valuable time on frivolous matters. A real man is not too proud to say "I need a hand," while at the same time being always willing to lend one. A real man does not measure himself by his career, his salary, or the number of women he's "screwed." A real man lives with integrity.

Let's talk, too, about the need for black men to "be strong." We tell each other to "be strong" all the time. What do we really mean when we say that? We have to be careful when we tell our brothers to "be strong"—especially our youth. If we are not careful, we may send the wrong message to them. They may interpret our words to mean that they must *always* be pillars of strength, never accepting their vulnerabilities. To "be strong" actually means to have a complete sense of who we truly are, being self-assured—not to be stubborn or "macho." So, when we tell ourselves and our brothers to "be strong," remember this.

He who sets out to achieve total masculinity can never fulfill his artificial ideal of being "man enough." Masculinity is simply what we expect of a man. When we mess up our lives—and possibly those of our wives and children—in our quest to feel "man enough," we are not exercising true masculinity, but a ludicrous exaggeration of what manhood is.

Action Steps

- Take care of your family. Nurture and cherish it.

- Be responsible for your own actions.

- Be a good listener and consider the plight of others with compassion.

- Be yourself. Being "macho" is outdated and overrated. It's foolish, and it can kill you.

- Don't be intimidated by a woman who earns more money or has a better education than you. She's one more of us who is succeeding. Cheer her on. If she's single, she might be a good catch!

- Read the book *Man Enough: Fathers, Sons, and the Search for Masculinity*, by Frank Pittman, M.D.

33. Never be too proud to ask for help.

I'm not afraid to ask anybody for anything I don't know.
Why should I be afraid? I'm trying to get somewhere. Help
me, give me direction. Nothing wrong with that.

—Michael Jordan, athlete

When was the last time you asked for help? What seems like
the hardest thing for some men to do is so very simple. Many
of us have come to believe that when we ask for help—no
matter how badly we need it—we are admitting weakness.
No man likes to feel he is vulnerable. "I'm a man. I don't
need any help," we say. Well, remember this, brother, first
you're a human; you're a man second. That means you
cannot do everything or know everything, and even *you* require and depend on others every now and then. The brave,
strong, and exceptional brother acknowledges his mortal lim-
itations.

Almost every day, men of color find themselves having to
prove their abilities and strengths. Yet, in our battle we must
be cautious in projecting hard or superhero images. They can
work against us.

When our sisters and children offer to help us cope with
personal or work-related problems, they're not challenging
our manhood, they are showing their support and desire to
see us achieve. When coworkers extend helping hands with a
particular task you have been assigned, jump at the offer; two
heads are often better than one. Drop the played-out male-
ego routine, brother, and accept folks' offer of helping hands.
It may save you valuable time and energy. Listen and watch
them attentively; you just might learn a thing or two.

A heart full of senseless pride does not prove our manhood. The "bigger" man is the one who is able to confidently
say: "I just don't know . . ." "I can't seem to get this
to . . . ," or "I need a little help with this."

So, go ahead, be a man. Put your ego aside and have the strength to ask for help when you need it. You'll be a better man for it.

Action Steps

- Ask for directions if you're lost. It will save you valuable time, and no one will condemn you for it.

- If you're feeling guilty, talk to the Creator, your pastor, or your priest to confess and seek forgiveness.

- When driving, if you get sleepy, simply pull over to a safe place to park to rest your eyes. It's okay—really.

- See a doctor if you're having trouble getting aroused by your partner during sexual activity. More than likely, it is a medical problem that can be easily fixed, allowing you to once again enjoy lovemaking to the capacity that you want.

- Ask for an explanation when you don't understand something. This goes for questions you have in the classroom, on the job, or on the tennis court. There is no such thing as a stupid question if the information will enlighten and help you. Asking is the smart thing to do. Remember, it's better to ask first than to screw it up because your pride got in the way.

34. Speak up to injustice.

*Rise, brothers! . . . Never say: "Let well enough alone."
. . . Be discontented. . . . Let your discontent break
mountain-high against the wall of prejudice, and swamp it
to the very foundation. Then we shall not have to plead for
justice nor on bended knee crave mercy; for we shall be
men.*

—John Hope, educator

People of color face injustice daily. We know that. It is something we live with but must not accept. Many of us have been the target of a racial slur or a discriminatory act at some point in our lives. If we are to live full lives, men, we cannot and should not allow injustice to have a place in society.

It is so important to remember that as we march toward justice and equality, we should not speak up against injustice only when *we* are affected. The Rev. Dr. Martin Luther King Jr. once said that "injustice anywhere is a threat to justice everywhere." If you hear or see someone else being berated, intimidated, or just plain being treated wrong because of who or what he or she is, stand up and say something. Stand up and do something about it. Be an agitator. Make your opposition known by making some noise! When wrongful actions unnerve us, we must always challenge them head-on. When we sit in silence, at that moment we are condoning the ugly act.

Here's a story worth noting: It was Ron's first day on the job with a new company. There he overheard a white male coworker telling a joke on the telephone:

JOKER: "Now that Tiger Woods has twice won the Masters, have you heard what they're renaming the tournament?
JOKEE: "No. What?"
JOKER: "The Slaves."

Clearly, this was disturbing to Ron, a descendant of slaves. It should be to anyone. Ron spoke up. He told his supervisor what he overheard, and that he was offended by the racist joke. He told her it made him feel uncomfortable and angry, and that he thought action should be taken to address the matter. The supervisor later spoke to Ron's coworker who, in turn, apologized about the matter, explaining that he meant nothing by it. By Ron's raising the issue with someone in charge, the workers in the predominantly white office environment will now think twice about cracking jokes about people who look different from themselves.

Some black folks might have kept mum, deciding not to rock the boat—especially on the first day of a new job. However, keeping silent would have condoned the joke. Ron earned a greater respect from all of those in the office who appreciated being made aware that some things may be fun and frolic to them, but are insensitive to others. That afternoon, Ron and his coworker discussed the matter in private. They were able to continue their professional relationship and, at the same time, enlighten each other by frequently discussing other sensitive black-white issues over lunch.

Action Steps

- Speak up for equal rights and justice, even when doing so is not popular.

- Talk with Caucasian friends and coworkers about ethnic backgrounds to better understand each other's differences.

- Write or call your public officials with your opinions on legislation affecting justice and equal rights; don't wait for someone else to do it for you.

35. Show *yourself* the money.

I would always say that I wanted to be somebody who made history. I didn't want to be a man who just lived and died. I made up my mind early that I was going to be successful, a multimillionaire.

—Sean "P. Diddy" Combs, entertainer

There are some major benefits to owning your own enterprise: You call your own shots, decide your own work hours,
and take vacations when you want. Still, with every type of
freedom comes responsibility, and economic freedom
through entrepreneurship is no exception.

Off the bat, you should determine whether you have what
it takes—discipline, commitment, and endurance—to be an
entrepreneur. You must also be willing to take risks. A major
risk is often not knowing if, when, or from where your next
paycheck will come. We know, however, that without risks
we do not grow or prosper; nothing ventured, nothing
gained—as the saying goes.

Those who do not try, never make it. Just think about African Americans like the late A. G. Gaston, an Alabama busi-
nessman who amassed a fortune worth $40 million. Think
about John Johnson, the publishing tycoon. Both these men
built empires with modest dollars—and without the help of
affirmative action programs.

Most importantly, we should understand that showing
yourself the money is important because traditional sources
of income for African Americans are drying up. No longer
can we or should we rely solely upon the benefits of the
"secure" federal-government jobs our parents landed right
out of high school. With newer and faster technology developing every day, more and more computers and other de-
vices are replacing people on the job. The information age
our parents never dreamed of is here—ready or not.

Action Steps

- Start a small business with only reliable colleagues who share
your entrepreneurial spirit and interests.

- Research the pros and cons of opening a business. Consider
all the sacrifices, such as time with your spouse or mate and
your children.

- Consider investing dollars in African American–owned businesses.

- If you've mastered a skill on the job, take that skill and open your own firm—many companies, including the one you leave, may contract out work to you.

- Subscribe to *Black Enterprise* magazine.

36. Eat a healthy diet.

Whatsoever was the father of disease, an ill diet was the mother.

—Unknown

These days, it seems everything that tastes good is bad for you. Pork makes our "pressure" rise. (There go the chitlins.) Fried foods are greasy, increasing our cholesterol levels. (There go the fish fries.) Cakes and pies are loaded with fat and sugar, putting the pounds on us. (There go Ms. Eloise's fudge brownies.)

There are many theories about black men's susceptibility to certain illnesses, with the primary theories being diet-related. Traditional Southern food—as tasty as it is—is often higher in cholesterol, fat, salt, and sugar than are contemporary dishes. While it is true African Americans hail from all over the nation, at one time or another most of our ancestors lived in the South. As slaves, they were forced to creatively cook the leftover "scraps" from the big house. The Southern style of cooking was carried on with many of our people as they migrated north, east, and west following the abolishment of slavery.

However, in our quest for better lives, we overlooked changing what and how we eat. We continued to cook with our salt pork, fatback, and lard. We also continued to eat our ribs and pig feet. We call it soul food. Most of us have heard the oft-told story of one's uncle who was always a "meat 'n' potatoes man" and was never sick a day in his life—died at a ripe old age. Well, times have changed, research has expanded. Now we know that his diet wasn't the reason he lived so long, and that there are better ways to eat.

Many men (particularly single ones) who lead the no-cooking lifestyle, and families who claim they're too busy to cook, dine too frequently on fast-food meals. They "swing by and pick something up on the way home," only to serve sodium-laden hamburgers, french fries, milkshakes, chicken fingers, or TV dinners. We pave the path for all kinds of cardiovascular trouble with a diet like this.

Well, fellas, it's time to adjust our attitudes about cooking and eating. Our lives depend on it. We must prepare and eat our food in a more healthful way. We should not always fry our foods—we should bake, broil, or grill those meats. Stop tipping the salt shaker and "wake up" those veggies and pasta dishes with palate-pleasing herbs and spices, like curry or rosemary. Cook those collards and mustards with turkey legs—not ham hocks. Drink skim or 1 percent milk, and "butter up" those yams with cholesterol-free vegetable oil or margarine, not butter.

Now that's not to say you cannot ever indulge in a nice juicy steak, your dad's homemade chess pie, a meat-lover's pizza, or an onion ring or two. As with anything, though, do it in moderation—that is the key. Ironically, too much of a good thing is usually bad for you.

Eating a healthy, sensible diet, coupled with a regular exercise routine, can help to ward off cardiovascular disease diabetes, high blood pressure, and even certain types of cancer. Most of all, bro, it will change how you look, feel, and live.

It's sad, but, if you think about it, we are often more concerned with what type of gas and oil we put into our cars than we are about what we put into our own bodies.

Now, chew on that. . . .

Action Steps

- Buy a book on good health. Three recommended titles are *The Black Man's Guide to Good Health*, by James W. Reed, M.D., Neil B. Shulman, M.D., and Charlene Shucker; *Good Health for African Americans*, by Barbara Dixon; and *Make the Connection*, by Oprah Winfrey and Bob Greene. They're great reads for helping you lead a physically healthier life.

- Pick up two good books: 1) *The Healthy Soul Food Cookbook*, by Wilbert Jones; and 2) *The New Soul Food Cookbook for People With Diabetes*, by Fabiola Demps Gaines and Roniece Weaver. Books such as these are packed with healthful, but tasteful, recipes!

- Next time you are at the grocery store, instead of making a beeline for the chips, grab the grapes. These and other fresh fruits, like bananas, apples, and oranges, are not only good for you, they make great snacks for you, the family, and guests.

- Eat more fresh vegetables: sweet potatoes or yams, greens, broccoli, cauliflower, carrots, and spinach. Also, when preparing them, make sure they are done, but don't cook all the nutrients out. (Black folks have a history of cooking our vegetables down until they're limp and less nutritious.) Five servings of fruits and vegetables per day should be your average consumption.

- Eat lots of whole-grain breads, rice, and cereals. Eating foods high in fiber wards off certain types of cancer, is good for the digestive system, and keeps you "regular."

- Do away with the dairy. About 60 to 75 percent of adult African Americans have an extremely high lactose-intolerance for dairy products. Whole milk, cheese, butter, and ice cream may just be what's "doing a number" on your stomach, and you don't even know it.

- Limit your intake of red meat and pork. Eat more fish and chicken, but bake, don't fry.
- Throw away your grease can!
- Plan meals ahead of time for yourself and your family.
- Take your lunch to work. Research shows that a person who eats out every workday (five days a week) spends on average $200 a month. Besides, you can plan and eat more healthful meals by "brown-bagging it."
- Encourage your mate, friends, and family members to eat a more healthy diet and to exercise regularly.

37. Help to keep the women in your life breast-healthy.

Hindsight explains the injury that foresight would have prevented.

—Unknown

The women in our lives are special to us. Our wives. Ladyfriends. Sisters. Mama. Nana. Aunt Helen. That is why it is so important for us to take an interest in their physical well-being. We all want to keep our loved ones around for years to come, so let's do our part—especially when it comes to their breast health.

Every three minutes a woman somewhere in the United States is diagnosed with breast cancer. Every eleven minutes a woman dies of the disease. According to the American Cancer Society, an estimated 192,200 cases of invasive breast cancer would be diagnosed in 2001. Sadly, some studies have shown that in the United States, African-American women in their forties are known to have a 30 to 50 percent higher breast-cancer mortality rate than white women. Breast tumors in black women are consistently diagnosed at a more advanced stage of the disease. Black men can help out by reminding black women that they should be checked out—sooner rather than later. Health experts say failure to seek early detection and a lack of awareness and education often lead to more serious cases—some of which could have been treated better if caught earlier.

For years, all women were urged to have an annual mammogram (an x-ray of the breast) beginning at age forty. In 1996 health officials of the National Cancer Institute, American Cancer Society, National Black Women's Health Project (NBWHP), and National Institutes of Health began scrambling hard to determine at what stage early detection is most successful. In a woman's forties? Her fifties? In 1997 the NBWHP maintained that mammography screening doesn't seem to help younger women because they tend to develop a more aggressive, rapid-growing form of breast cancer that mammography screening doesn't detect. Also, the Project's experts say *they* have not seen data indicating that screening for women under fifty—especially women under forty-five—will pick up cancers. NBWHP experts say more research into diagnostic tools is required.

Right now is a very confusing time for health-care officials and medical researchers. They have, in essence, said they do not yet have all the answers. So it's even more mind-boggling for our women. What's a woman to do? How can the men in her life best support her?

Well, as with other health matters, education helps pave the way to prevention. So, educating ourselves is our first step. In addition, we must not be shy about talking with our own doctors about our mates' health and well-being. Let us start by reading up on the latest findings about breast cancer. We can also do our part by staying informed and encouraging the special ladies in our lives to get the facts on how best to protect and preserve their bodies.

Action Steps

- Get the facts about cancer awareness and prevention. Your local health department and/or doctor's office should have pamphlets on these topics. While you are there, specifically request a breast self-exam shower hanger (a plastic, water-resistant, die-cut card that hangs on the showerhead) for your loved one. On the card are simple instructions on how to do a breast self-exam during a shower.

- Ask your loved one if she gets routine checkups. If not, ensure that she (or you) schedules her appointment as soon as possible. Tell her you are asking because you care about and love her. It's not about being shy to talk to a woman about her body. Both of you, get over it! It's about possibly saving her life!

- Find out where the women you love and care about can get a *free* or low-cost mammogram and Pap test by calling the Center for Disease Control and Prevention at 1-888-842-6355.

- Ensure your loved one does as *you* should be doing—visiting the doctor for regular checkups. A breast exam and a Pap test (for cervical cancer) are two pertinent screenings for deadly cancers.

- Know that men develop breast cancer, too, although we account for less than 1 percent of cases. According to the American Cancer Society, an estimated 1,500 cases were projected to have been diagnosed in 2001. Early detection saved the life of actor Richard ("Shaft") Roundtree, who strongly urges brothers to be better in tune with their bodies.

- Be sure to check out the National Cancer Institute's Cancer Information Center's Web site at http://cancernet.nci.nih.gov

- To learn more about mammography risks and benefits, write the National Women's Health Network, 514 Tenth St., N.W., Ste. 400, Washington, DC 20004. Other resources include the National Cancer Institute (800-4-CANCER), and the American Cancer Society (800-ACS-2345).

- Share your cancer information with your loved ones. They and you will be glad you did.

- Check out a wealth of women's health information on the National Women's Health Information Center Web site at http://www.4women.gov

38. Have the courage to say "I'm sorry."

Learn to speak kind words. Nobody resents them.

—Carl Rowan, journalist

"I'm sorry." It takes a big man to say these two little words. Yet some men just can't fix their mouths to say them.

Wise is the man who is willing to accept responsibility for his wrongdoing. Some brothers go through life with no apologies, no remorse. Admitting mistakes is not about giving in, being weak, or losing a battle. It's about finding the courage to right the wrong, seek forgiveness, and move on to resolution. So, have the courage to give an apology when you're wrong, brother. If you don't have it to give, then you can't expect to get it back. That's the law of reciprocity.

Action Steps

- When letting others know how you feel, don't use the accusatory "you," such as: "You always . . . ," "You did . . . ," etc. Phrases like: "I feel . . . " and "I felt . . ." come across as less threatening and invite opportunity for resolution, rather than defensiveness.

- Free your relationships of power struggles and ego trips, and master the art of apologizing.

- Buy or rent the video documentary *Sister, I'm Sorry—An Apology to Our African-American Queens,* coproduced by actor Blair Underwood. Intended as an atonement by African-American men toward their female counterparts, it features eight women who convey moving, real-life accounts of rape, abuse, incest, and abandonment. Underwood and fellow actors Michael Beach and Tommy Ford are among the brothers who apologize. Curl up and view it with the woman in your life!

- Stop it before it even gets to "I'm sorry."

- Know that an apology never diminishes a man; it elevates him.

39. Stand for something.

A man who stands for nothing will fall for anything.
—Malcolm X, civil-rights leader

It's easy to say you believe in something. But what do you stand for? The genuine work begins when you incorporate real meaning behind your belief. Statements like "I feel . . ." "I believe . . ." "In my opinion . . ." tell folks what you're saying, but not necessarily what you're doing.

Perhaps you stand for nonviolence, better public schools, cancer prevention, world peace, or freedom of lifestyle choice. All this is well and good, but you need to take what you stand for and not stand still—march toward making it reality.

Action Steps

- Write down what you feel strongly about and why; then get busy pursuing your cause.
- Don't get bogged down in every cause. Too much time spent on too many causes makes your overall effort halfhearted and produces little impact on anything.
- Share your stance with others, but never force your personal beliefs and opinions upon others.

40. Respect authority.

There is an exception to every rule—and most people think they are it.

—Unknown

Obey the law. Observe the rules. Seems like such orders should go without saying. Most of us have an early memory of learning the meaning of the words *no, can't,* and *don't.* Yet some folks simply have no respect for authority—whether it be for a boss, parent, teacher, police officer, or the like.

Even responsible adults sometimes decide to go against the grain, go against the law. Case in point: Each year, countless young black men are killed because of disregard for the law. We live in a society governed by established rules and regulations, and we must abide by them.

Sometimes we feel strongly that certain "rules and regs" are unfair, unjust, unreasonable. Well, then we must put ourselves in a position to make our voices heard to bring about changes civilly. For one man, it is through exercising his right to vote. For another, it may be through contacting the lawmakers themselves. Still, for others, it may be through getting elected to public office.

Until such changes can be accomplished, have respect for

authority. There are enough of us already in trouble with the law.

Action Steps

- Instill in your children and the ones you mentor the importance of respecting authority.

- Use the phrase "Do as I say, not as I do" cautiously with children. Be sure to practice what you preach.

- When seeking an opportunity, and someone tells you no, you say "Next!" Don't take no for an answer. Always seize the opportunity that will take you higher.

41. Always project a good image.

What you see is what you get!
—Flip Wilson, entertainer

Brother Flip was right. Most of us get what we see. We must also give others the best of what to see.

We should always project a good image by carrying ourselves the way most of us want to be perceived—in the highest regard. How you look and what you sound like are paramount to projecting a good image. You've heard the saying, "His reputation precedes him"? Well, so does yours.

Action Steps

- If your car windows are down, turn down the car stereo; you're being rude. Plus, what makes you think others want to hear your music over their own?

- Don't wear a 'do rag,' plastic moisturizer cap, or stocking cap on your head in public. Hair care should take place inside the home or at the hair salon. There's nowhere you have to go so quickly that you can't take that off your head.

- Stop cussing; you're perceived as vile and having a limited vocabulary. Cussing like a sailor doesn't prove your masculinity—it proves your ignorance.

- Speak plainly and articulately; you'll be perceived as being intelligent.

- Dress for the occasion. There's nothing like a well-dressed man.

- Lose the big-daddy pimp walk and quit grabbing your crotch. You look ridiculously insecure about your manhood.

42. Practice good etiquette.

You can dress 'em up, but you cain't take 'em out!
—African-American saying

Being able to conduct yourself in an appropriate manner will certainly enhance your chances for success.

For example, be on time for all appointments. Running on "colored people's time"—or CPT as we call it among ourselves—went out of style years ago. Being casually late has never really been in vogue.

Simple words like *thank you, please,* and *excuse me* are always appropriate and should be part of your everyday vocabulary.

Equally important is knowing things like which fork to use during dinner—at home and in public—and what to wear for a job interview.

If you don't know what is suitable or fitting for a particular occasion or purpose, make it your business to find out. The payoff is big, buddy.

Action Steps

- Add to your home library hardcover copies of the books *How To Be,* by Harriette Cole; *Basic Black,* by Karen Grigsby Bates and Karen E. Hudson; and *How to Be a Gentleman,* by John Bridges. Real men are comfortable with traditional etiquette—from writing thank-you notes to selecting a bottle of wine. These books are excellent contemporary-etiquette guides, preparing brothers for every occasion—something we need to work on.

- Be punctual, and insist on punctuality in others. For example, if your barbershop has lines for days, you might consider choosing one that takes appointments. By the way, never wait for more than fifteen minutes for a barber to call you to the chair. Your time is just as valuable as the barber's.

- If you are unsure about what to say, what to wear, or how to properly proceed, ask someone whom you admire and respect for his keen sense of always knowing the appropriate thing to do.

- When dining out, don't be a cheap tipper. It doesn't become you!

- At the gym: Don't hog the weights, return the weights to the weight rack, and remove plates from the bars when you're done; bring a towel to wipe your sweat off the equipment after you use it, and pick up after yourself.

- Chivalry is *not* dead. Brother, hold the door for the sister! Help the sister with her coat! Pull the sister's chair for her at the dinner table! And offer her your seat on the train!

43. Love yourself.

To enjoy a lifetime of romance, fall in love with yourself.

—Proverb

It may seem self-centered to say love yourself, but really it is not. The first and foremost person who is responsible for you is you. Y-O-U. This is not something we should take lightly. Often we make sure we love others, but in the process we forget to love ourselves.

There is nothing wrong with looking out for yourself. Tony, a thirtysomething brother, lives by the slogan "Take thee care of number one." While this doesn't mean forget the world, it does mean what it plainly says.

The rationalization is quite simple. You may have a heart to want to help others, but if you don't take care of yourself first, you will be in no shape to help anybody.

So remember, love yourself. Do things to make yourself happy, as peace of mind is a major part of loving yourself.

Action Steps

- Treat your body as a temple: Care for it and respect it. It's the only one you have.
- Treat yourself to a personal shopping spree.
- Remember to do the things that make you happy.
- Give yourself a pat on the back every now and then.

44. Be grateful.

> *If you concentrate on what you have, you'll end up having more. If you concentrate on what you don't have, you'll never have enough—that's a guarantee.*
>
> —Oprah Winfrey, media tycoon and entertainer

Oprah shared this kernel of wisdom with her talk-show viewers during a program on which the importance of gratitude was discussed. Later in the show, the sister quoted thirteenth-century prophet Meister Eckhart, who was known for his profound moral insight. He said: "If the only prayer you say in your entire life is 'Thank you,' it will be enough." These words can speak to each of us personally, making us ask ourselves, "How often do I say only a thank-you prayer?" Most of us ask, ask, and ask again for the things we want in life. Sometimes we get them. Sometimes we don't. Again, how often do we set aside our wants and desires during quiet time with the Creator just to say how grateful we are for the things we have been given. For most of us, not nearly as often as we should.

We spend most of our lives reaching for "the good life." We want safe, comfortable homes for ourselves and our families, food in our bellies, clothes on our backs, good mental and physical health, freedom of choice, successes in our careers—just to name a few. So in reality, a man's needs are quite basic. If and when our desires manifest—ones that stem from our oft-instant-gratitude pleas—we, in turn, should "hustle butt" to give thanks, each in his own way.

Stop and take a minute to jot down five things for which you are grateful. Perhaps your list includes: Your wife's love and support. Fresh air. Books. The guidance and wisdom your grandfather gave you as a young boy. Good sex. Weekends. Your newborn son. Classical music. The Chicago Bulls. Universal remote controls. Your spirituality. Big Mama's sweet potato pie. E-mail. Your PalmPilot.

Today, start a gratitude journal in which you record each day at least five things for which you are grateful. Log those things for which you are thankful, not what you think others want to read should you choose to share your journal with them. Scrawl across as many pages as it takes. Your journal doesn't need to be fancy. It can be a blank-page hardback, a simple spiral notebook, or a yellow legal pad. Maybe your gratitude moment will be spent in front of your computer, keying in your list. Whatever—list anything you want, be brief or lengthy, but just be honest.

Most folks are happy to have been blessed with certain things they have. From time to time, some of us even take them for granted. Remember the saying, "You can't take it with you"? So, give thanks while you have it. Just be prepared and willing to part with it. As fast as it's given, it can be taken away.

Oprah's words on gratitude should give us all a lot to think about. They should make us think about the way we place value on what we have versus what we need. We can all start our own gratitude journals, logging daily. Some older brothers have been journaling for years. Many report that recording their thoughts has changed their lives. It will change yours.

Get busy writing, brotherman.

Action Steps

- Give thanks before each meal, no matter how big or small.

- Encourage the entire family to keep gratitude journals and schedule sharing times.

- Tell others "thank you" when they go out of their way to give you a hand.

- Write and send thank-you notes in response to gifts and kindnesses you receive from others. And teach your children to do the same.

45. Take time out for self-service.

It's no disgrace to start over or to begin anew.
—Bebe Moore Campbell, journalist and author

Sometimes we need to just open our eyes. We can usually see everyone's flaws but our own.

Most of us like to think we're fine just the way we are. Fact is, however, we all can use a little reengineering from time to time. Some men are long overdue, but have no idea where to begin. The good part is we have a home-court advantage, since we know ourselves better than anyone else. Like the cars that we drive, most of us sense when it's time for servicing.

Taking time out to care for ourselves can present a clear picture of the problems that exist. It allows us to discover which attitudes need adjusting, ways need mending, and outlooks need retooling. We must ask ourselves questions like: "On what areas do I need work?" and "What can I do to make me run like new?" Recording our answers on paper gives us an itemized list of repairs and adjustments to be made. Set aside time this week to write up your maintenance ticket. It could be time for a tune-up.

Action Steps

- Assess your personal attitudes and beliefs. Are they current or archaic?

- Update your résumé and career portfolio this week.

- Go ahead and get rid of your gray hair if it makes you feel better about yourself.

- Finally go after the body you've been craving for yourself by starting and sticking to a healthy diet and workout plan.

- Begin a hair-regrowth program. Rogaine or Propecia just may be what you need to end the ongoing, torturous battle with your thinning hair.

- If you're impotent, ask your doctor about whether or not the "wonder drug" Viagra is a viable solution for you.

- Take an assertiveness class at the local community college to help boost your self-esteem.

- Assess your spirituality.

46. Spend only a modest amount of money playing your lottery numbers.

Play responsibly. It's all about fun!

—Seen on the back of a lottery ticket

Some brothers spend a small fortune playing their "numbers" in hopes of hittin' it big one day. They think very little about the incredible odds against winning.

Most of us can recall seeing brothers (and sisters) standing in long lottery lines at the corner liquor store, carryout, or gas station. We play 'em all—three-way, four-way, Lotto, Big Game, Powerball. We also know all the combinations—a dollar-straight, fifty-cents backup, boxed, six-dollar combo. Well, at least we know what we're playing and where our money is going. Seriously, when we overspend our hard-earned dollars playing the lottery we run the dangerous risk of becoming "lottery poor" in the process.

Many a brother dreams of hitting the numbers jackpot and livin' large. Unfortunately, most everyone who plays can't win. True, you can't win if you don't play. Just be sure you're not betting all your money on a lottery pipe dream.

Action Steps

- "I'm not hooked," you say? Well, if you play religiously, don't play any lottery games or gamble otherwise for the next two weeks. You will survive. Put those dollars in the bank, buy a good book, or pay off a small bill. You'll test your willpower, and you could keep a few extra dollars in your wallet.

- If you do play, complete your play cards *before* you get up to the cash register. Have respect for others waiting in line behind you.

- Don't take those lottery "dream books" seriously. Remember, they're for entertainment purposes only.

- On a related note: Limit the amount of time you spend playing the slot and video-poker machines and crap tables in the casinos. Take a designated amount of spending money with you, and leave home *without* the ATM, credit and check cards!

47. Learn to handle your anger responsibly.

When a man angers you, he controls you.

—Toni Morrison, author

Of all the emotions we try to suppress, anger is not usually one of them. In fact, it's one of the few emotions many brothers feel they can express with confidence in front of others without the fear of being labeled as weak. When we're angry, we usually have an overwhelming feeling of helplessness, powerlessness, and even a loss of independence.

While anger is a normal emotion, we must check how we respond to it. We can respond in one of three ways: 1. Sit back and do nothing—a choice that may make us feel our needs and rights have been trampled on; 2. Explode in a rage— violently trespassing on the needs and rights of others; or 3. Express our own needs and rights without violating the needs and rights of others in the process.

Sometimes we find ourselves wavering between numbers 1 and 2, but wise is the man who knows that choosing either does not lessen his anger; nor does it make him a stronger or nobler man. As intelligent and responsible brothers, we have got to opt for number 3.

When we are angry, sometimes our ability to reason becomes clouded. However, we must not confuse aggressiveness with assertiveness. Aggressiveness is an inclination to act in a hostile way—dominating, manipulating, or using force. Assertiveness is the bold inclination to assert yourself with confidence and self-assurance.

Some brothers grew up with anger expressed physically in their homes. Unfortunately, some of these men have carried on that tradition within their own households. Physical violence is not the answer to resolving any situation that challenges us. When we resort to responding in this way, it can mean innocent people get hurt or killed.

We are not controlled by others, nor can we control what others do. We can, however, control how we *react* to others' actions. When we handle our own anger in an assertive and positive way, we travel the "high road" of letting go, moving on.

Remember, what you do with your anger partly determines the kind of man you are. . . .

Action Steps

- Never go to bed angry.
- Next time you get angry at someone, instead of exploding in a rage, take a deep breath and go for a walk to cool off.
- Talk to a friend about what you're feeling inside.
- While you may not be able to forget, you have to learn to forgive. Harboring anger and resentment takes too much of your personal time and energy—energy that could be positively spent doing something that benefits you.
- Never fuss or fight with your wife in front of your children; it can skew their view about their parents and relationships. Work out your differences nonviolently in private.

- Learn about the difference between arguing and debating; then teach it to your children.

- Count to ten next time you feel like you're about to go off on someone. If you're really angry, continue counting to twenty-five.

- Write down your anger in a personal journal, if you keep one.

- Drop the grudge and replace it with pleasant memories.

48. Keep a journal.

The key to understanding others is to first understand yourself.

—Unknown

Did you know that one of the best things we can do for ourselves is to keep a daily journal? Yep. Logging those personal thoughts and reflections allows us to see ourselves more clearly, become more self-aware of who we are, where we have been, and where we're going. Awareness is an important part of any behavior change.

If you haven't done so, today is a good day to begin keeping your journal. Incorporate the activity into your morning and evening "me" time before heading to work and before bedtime. Once you begin, you'll quickly discover that keeping a journal will serve as one of the most important parts on your path to discovering your best self. The rewards are many. In the process, you will learn a great deal about your patterns, what causes you to say the things you say and do the things you do.

A journal or log need not be leather bound or fancy. It can simply be a spiral notebook, a three-ring binder filled with paper, or small pad. Of course, your local bookstore has an assortment of handsome journals on which you can even have your name engraved. How about a computerized journal you can keep on diskette? Do whatever works for you. In fact, your *daily* journal could double as your gratitude journal—you know, that book in which you should be recording daily at least five things for which you're grateful. Discover what works for you.

As you begin your journal, above all, be honest. Spill out your soul, tell it like it is. Know that there's no one to impress here, since this is for your eyes only. Remember, if you cheat, you're only deceiving yourself.

Log in the low you experienced when your manager made that snide comment today. The joy you felt when you brought your wife and newborn baby home from the hospital. The anger that bubbled inside you when your health-insurance rates notice arrived today. Recount the father-son times you had with Dad before he died. Reflect on your day. Jot down your personal goals for the new millennium. Generate a list of your strengths and weaknesses. Write down daily affirmations; when they're on paper, they seem more real. Write out what options you have in your current relationship. Plan what you'll say to your kids when it's time to discipline them. Map out the plays for the Little League team you got talked into coaching this season. Draft that love letter your "main squeeze" has been asking you to finally write her (after she heard about the idea on *Oprah*).

Keeping a journal brings us the clarity we need when life gets out of focus. It provides the comfort we need when another human can't. It serves as a compass to guide us when we're disoriented, lights our way to progress in the dark times. But its benefits don't stop there. Studies have shown that recording your thoughts and feelings helps to fire up your immune system, calm you down, and keep you healthy.

Most of us have so many other people's voices in our

heads on a given day that we barely hear our own. A journal is the perfect place to let yourself be heard. It won't interrupt or talk back to you, and it's great for sounding off.

Begin your journal today, chief. You will see progress.

Action Steps

- Check out the cool line of journals in the bookstore today.
- Share your journal with your mate if you choose, or keep it for your eyes only.
- Consider consolidating your daily journal and gratitude journal.
- Keep your log in a safe place.
- When writing your words, don't worry about spelling or grammar.
- When you don't feel like logging in, don't. Come back to it when you're ready.
- Review your journal entries periodically to measure your progress in altering your life.

49. Make a difference.

What I want to do is make a difference . . . Whether it's in the field of education or social services, what is most important, that I have a platform and an opportunity to bring about fundamental change.

—Ken Chenault, chairman and chief executive officer of American Express

Think back to the last time you made a difference for someone, for something, or for yourself. How did it make you feel? Perhaps you helped a young person meet her goal of selling candy in order to win the first-place prize by buying a box or two. Maybe you took an elderly relative to the eye doctor to finally get those new prescription glasses he's been needing, but had no way to get there. Or maybe you simply watered a wilted plant only to watch it sprout new leaves a few days later.

Our kind and loving acts need not be Nobel Prize–winning ones. They may even go unnoticed. Those of the anonymous kind are often the most fruitful for us and those who benefit. By the way, don't forget to allow *yourself* to be on the receiving end sometimes!

Action Steps

- Look at the man in the mirror and challenge him to start making a difference today.
- Be a positive impact on your environment, at work and at play.
- Don't be selfish; spread some of your expertise to others to make a change.

50. Simplify your life.

I don't know if I'm coming or going.

—American saying

We're often told to KISS (Keep It Short [and] Simple.) What good advice—especially these days.

During the busy course of things, we often get tied up here, tied up there. Then, before we know it, life is in complete chaos. It can make our heads spin. The only way to fully enjoy life and the abundance it holds is to be able to see life. Like a cluttered room or a disheveled desk, a life that is disorganized and complex will not be functional. Repeated close calls wear on the mind, the body, the spirit. As long as we keep "living hard," we'll continue to fall victim to helter-skelter circumstance.

There's the saying "If it ain't one thing, it's two." Ain't that the truth? Start today to simplify your life. You'll soon discover that you can deal with the day a heck of a lot easier!

Action Steps

- Keep your keys in the same place every day. They'll always be right there when you need them.

- Organize your papers (bills, letters, business cards, newspaper clippings, etc.).

- Get computerized to better organize your finances, address book, household inventory, etc.

- Use discretion when giving out your cell-phone number and e-mail address. Not everyone needs 24-7 access to you.

- Prepare food in bulk; portions can be frozen to heat when needed, saving lots of time and energy.

- Make daily to-do lists for household chores, and at work for assigned projects.

- Clean out the "junk drawer" in the kitchen.

- Keep a stationary pen and a notepad by every phone in the house.

- Organize your tools—when you need a screwdriver, you'll be able to find it.

- Label your videotapes right after you record on them.

- Clean you golf clubs immediately after your game. They will be ready and waiting for your next outing.

- Avoid being pickpocketed (and potentially painful buttock ailments later!) by *never* carrying your wallet in your pants pocket.

- Avoid long theater lines by ordering movie, opera, or stage-play tickets on-line via the Internet, or via telephone.

- At work: Watch loose talk in the bathroom. You never know who's in the stall and may overhear everything you say. Don't sleep with anyone who you can fire—or who can fire you.
- This week, take off your Superman cape.

51. Be able to "chew your tobacco twice."

The discreet man knows how to hold his tongue.

—Malagasy proverb

The man who can say something about someone behind his or her back, and can say it again to his or her face without fright, fear, or shame is a mighty big man.

Sometimes it's easy for words to roll right off our tongues without first giving them thought.

Let us think more about how abusive, disrespectful, or damaging words can be when we say things we'd rather not be repeated. Always be able to "chew your tobacco twice."

Action Steps

- Don't say things you really don't mean. White lies are *still* lies.
- Remember, you don't always have to have something to say.
- Choose your words wisely. You never know who's listening.

52. Choose carefully the company you keep.

*Align yourself with powerful people. Align yourself with
people that you can learn from, people who want more out
of life, people who are stretching and searching and
seeking some higher ground in life.*

—Les Brown, author and motivational speaker

Parents in the black community have always told us we are
judged by the company we keep, the friends with whom we
hang out, the fellas in our "posse." So true.

If you want to be seen as an upwardly mobile, progressive
brother who has his act together, it is not wise to be hanging
out with someone who has decided to move in the opposite
direction. Remember this:

If he's into dope, cut him from your rope.
If he's in a gang, don't hang.
If he's into abuse, he's no use.
If she has no plans, then make no plans to be with her.
If she steals, you know the deal—stay far away.

This is not to suggest that brothers should dis others. We
should simply rule out having any affiliation with brothers or
sisters who have decided that they will lead a life that attracts
ill will, things that could potentially bring us down. We can
try to help them move up, but if they choose not to progress,
we must move on and find better company to keep.

Action Steps

- Hang out with folks who have similar goals as you do.
- Release from your inner circle those who are "bad company."
- Develop new friendships with people who are positive.

53. Know it's okay to be happily *un*married.

Happiness is not having what you want. It's wanting what you have.

—Unknown

"So, when are you going to settle down?" is a question most marrying-age bachelors are constantly asked. Just what is the definition of "settle down," anyway? Contrary to popular belief, many of today's bachelors can cook tasty meals, care responsibly for their children, sew on their own buttons, keep clean homes, and launder clothes properly.

As a man approaches age thirty, if he is not married, he may unconsciously be held suspect by family and friends of being irresponsible, incapable of committing, gay, or all of the above. These are common stereotypes, but especially burdensome to black men—who are oft said to all be on drugs, in prison, or gay. However, many men today opt to go it alone. They are adopting babies, building their own homes, having rewarding careers, and maintaining happy, healthy unmarried relationships.

Unlike our fathers and grandfathers, today's brothers (and sisters, too) are waiting until later in life to marry—if they marry at all. While this may puzzle our elders, we must put them on notice that our marital status is, now more than ever, a personal choice. It is we who decide whether or not to walk down the aisle, exchange the vows, and toss the garter. Back in the day, "everyone" got married, made babies, and folks lived the "American Dream" (whatever that is supposed to be). It was the thing to do. Today, however, let us encourage those who are of that era to think about how the world and society have changed. The number of unmarried men and women continues to grow. In fact, the single life is becoming more socially acceptable and a viable alternative for some.

We have been "jumping the broom" since time began.

However, the notion of getting married in order to be "settled down" doesn't wash. It never has. So many men marry for the wrong reasons—they father a child prematurely, their families pressure them to find a "good woman" to take care of them, or they feel like it's "the corporate thing to do" in order to excel in the workplace. Many of those marriages don't make it. In the United States about 50 percent of all marriages end in divorce, with the main reasons being "incompatibility" and "irreconcilable differences." Conforming to traditions of society and its pressures does us little good. Brothers who rush to the altar for the wrong reasons cheat themselves and their mates.

It's true that most of us have a strong desire to share our lives with someone, but marriage is not the only answer to fulfillment. Our significant others, friends, and family members are also capable of filling that desire in many ways if we allow them.

They say married men live longer because they have someone looking out for them. Therefore, single brothers must engage in committed emotionally and physically healthy relationships. They don't, however, require legal papers and diamond rings to do so. There are things to be on the lookout for, though. Bachelors must be cognizant of sexual safety issues, such as AIDS and other sexually transmitted diseases. Men who are single and sexually active, must involve ourselves in monogamous relationships.

Many men today are discovering that bachelorhood can be just as rewarding as marriage is for their "wedlocked" counterparts. They are realizing that they, too, can lead full lives, understanding that bachelorhood doesn't equate with loneliness or being incomplete. Brothers who are educated and financially independent, in particular, are now realizing they are certainly free to be single and happy. They're discovering a freedom to experience life in a way no other generation of men has.

If you're single, know it's okay to not be or not want to be married. Don't let anyone tell you otherwise. Choosing to get married, or not to, is your decision. You don't need anyone to take care of you. Make that possible for yourself.

Action Steps

- Consider this: Are you a marrying type of guy? Take a moment or two to determine for yourself what relationship style makes *you* happy—not others who can't wait to throw birdseed, eat cake, and dance at your wedding. Are you a person who's better suited for a lifetime of marriage with your special someone? Are you someone who's most content in a unmarried-but-committed monogamous relationship with your special lady? Or are you content to live the "unhappily-married-and-just-date-the-honeys" lifestyle?

- Single brothers, the next time someone asks you when you're going to turn in your "player's card," simply and politely respond: "I'm bright, independent, positive, and settled. Best of all, I have choices. When or if I will marry I have yet to decide."

- If you're single or divorced and want to be a father, go ahead and adopt that baby or child(ren) you want. There are plenty little ones who need a loving home and caring parent.

- Single brothers, think about what qualities you possess that would make you a good husband or loving, responsible dad.

- If your child's mother is unjustly keeping him or her from you, fight for your right to play an active, loving fatherhood role. Empower yourself to seek the necessary legal representation, and network with and enlist the support of other men in your situation.

- Divorced gents, think about what you might do differently in a relationship should you decide to remarry.

54. Embrace computer technology.

The digital divide is about more than owning cell phones or pagers; it's about learning a new vocabulary—like dot-coms, E-commerce, distance learning, *and* broadband. *Those who don't understand these concepts or have no stake in their development will be digital have-nots, with limited access to knowledge and economic leverage.*

—William E. Kennard, former chairman of the
Federal Communications Commission

Absolutely! How many times have you heard our brothers and sisters say, "I don't know nothin' 'bout no computers!"? Many folks defensively claim they are "a people person," and that "computers make you lose the personal touch" with others. The reality is that these nonusers have decided not to *make* the time to broaden their knowledge base and find out how computers can actually *improve* their communication skills—not only one-on-one, but with the entire world. They don't realize that more-than-basic computer skills are necessary, especially in the workplace. Like a child who learns to overcome his fear of sleeping without the light on, so, too, must we overcome our fear of computers and other facets of technology.

Computers have become a part of our everyday lives inside and outside the home. Today, we not only use them to write letters and to play games, we also use them to: bank in the comfort of our pajamas in bed; send e-mail messages and digital colorful photos of the kids to family and friends around the world; produce colorful presentations at work; and jam to Jill Scott, rock with Billy Joel, or sway to the gospel sounds of Mahalia Jackson via built-in multimedia players. All this happens with clicks of a mouse and taps of keys. What's more, with the right software, one can even make long-distance calls around the world for free! The Internet is the largest part of the information superhighway. This network of computers puts you in touch with 30 to 40 million people across the globe. It is absolutely essential to get "plugged in and on-line" in this day and age.

No longer is it considered "nerdy" or "geeky" to know computers and take advantage of all they can do for you. If becoming computer-literate means reading the software and hardware manuals that came bundled with your computer, simply make the time to do it. If it means getting with a friend or cousin one day a week to get comfortable with computers, do it! Today, even our youngest children are surpassing adults with the computer literacy they are gaining in the classroom. Many of them are teaching *us* how to get on-line, to "open a window," and to "surf the Net."

In 2000, provisional research showed a little over half of all African Americans use computers, while 63 percent of whites use computers. Rural blacks are not nearly as connected to the Internet as blacks who live in cities or suburbs. The study also showed just 22 percent of blacks in rural areas have on-line access, compared to 41 percent of suburban blacks who have access and 35 percent of urban blacks. These studies of the "digital divide" have revealed that income, education, and residence explain the disproportionate low use of computers by blacks when compared to whites. Meanwhile, other research shows that 80 percent of black folks spend their hard-earned dollars on audio equipment.

If we African Americans are to survive as full participants in this society, we must understand and *apply* what works *now*. Otherwise, we will be left stranded on the technology on-ramp, waiting for someone to come rescue us with outdated software, nonupgradable hardware, and slow connections to the next technological phase. It's time to get it: Technology is no longer the wave of the future. In fact, it *always* has been the future, with blacks playing catch-up yet again. The time is now for us to embrace the technological fruits our anscestors could only dream of!

Action Steps

- Take a computer-literacy course at a community college or community center. Many classes are offered in the evenings or on the weekend to accommodate your busy workweek schedule.

- Subscribe to a commercial on-line service, such as America Online or Microsoft Network. These provide easy access to the Internet. Most services even offer you your own e-mail address(s) and the opportunity to build your own personal Web site.

- If you're already computer-literate, master all the software on your machine. Make an effort to learn one new software program a month. This way, you can start using the computer to your full advantage, instead of just to play Solitaire.

- If your are technically savvy, visit http://www.blackgeeks.com, a Web site that gives African Americans news about information technologies.

- If you own a business, ensure you have an Internet presence via a professional-looking Web site.

- If you don't have access to the Internet at home, access it for free at your local library.

- Realize that you should know basic computer terms like: *Windows, PC, hard drive, floppy disk, CD-ROM, download, chatting, mouse, browser,* and *MP3.* If you can't define these, brother, you've got some learning to do!

55. Smile.

*Not all of your scowling and fussing and growling can
show off your grit like a smile.*

—Unknown

For something that seems so easy, we often find smiling the
hardest thing to do. Never has something so little meant so
much. A smile can lift a mourning soul. A smile can light up
a child's face. A smile can turn a frown into a grin. A smile
can do so much, and it doesn't cost a thing. An old song sung
in Sunday school went something like this:

> You can smile,
>   When you can't say a word,
> You can smile,
>   When you cannot be heard,
> You can smile,
>   When it's cloudy or fair,
> You can smile anytime, anywhere.

Amen to that!

Plus, it takes more muscles to frown or make an ugly face
than it takes to smile. Also, according to experts like Dr. Su-
zanne Segerstrom, assistant professor with the Department of
Psychology at the University of Kentucky, smiling can have a
direct impact on how long you live. In a *People* magazine
article a few years ago, Segerstrom pointed out that her research showed that "having a positive outlook might increase the number of disease-fighting T-cells in your system,"
and that "your attitude may affect one or more levels of defense in the immune system."

Moreover, when you smile, people feel more comfortable with you. When you smile, you invite communication and cooperation. People are immediately aware that this is a person who may be helpful, whether it be professional or personal. Say cheese!

Action Steps

- Get your day off to a pleasant start: Smile at yourself when you look in the mirror in the morning.
- Smile at the first person you see today.
- If you encounter someone in a bad mood, smile at him or her; it may be just what's needed to lift his or her spirits.

56. Have a passion.

I believe you're here to live your life with a passion.
Otherwise you're just traveling through the world blindly—
and there's no point to that.

Oprah Winfrey, media tycoon and entertainer

Darrell is a forty-one-year-old M.D. who was bored with his job as a pediatrician. Although he made big bucks, was well respected in the medical community, and was praised for his leadership efforts on numerous boards, he didn't feel he was living to his fullest career potential. However, he just wasn't sure what career path would fill the void.

So, he took evening and weekend classes in everything he found remotely interesting—business administration, photography, theater, real estate. He ended up leaving his practice, altering his financial lifestyle, and going back to school to earn a master's degree in computer science from the Big Ten school at which his favorite football team plays. Changing careers after seven years of private practice, he now runs a successful computer-consulting firm which has managed to land major contracts with several corporations, government agencies, and community organizations in the city to which he moved. He also now gets to attend all the football games rather than watch them on TV. Darrell conquered his restlessness. Darrell didn't block his calling. Darrell found his passion.

There's something refreshing about watching someone who has a passion for what he does. You can see it in his eyes. Focus. Pride. Commitment. Dedication. Determination. You can feel it when you're in his presence. The energy fills the room. Most of us know someone like Darrell. The guy who pulls out all the stops, follows his true calling. He's the one who steps out on faith, makes monetary sacrifices, makes the necessary adjustments to succeed and be happy.

Sadly most people abandon their innermost aspirations when confronted with the disapproval (both harmless and harmful) of loved ones and friends. They compromise their ability to soar to success and instead flounder in mediocrity, all because of ill-gotten advice.

Zero in on that one thing that makes you happy, the thing that is most important to you.

When we have a true passion for what we're doing (engaging in a hobby, participating in a sport, or giving a hand up to the less fortunate in our community) it gives us validation, boosts our self-confidence, recharges our battery. Sometimes our true passion is right under our nose. Sometimes it's buried deep inside our soul and needs to be coaxed out. Let's remove our blinders to discover what we've been missing. What is your passion, chief? Gather your hunting gear, and start exploring today!

Action Steps

- Read *What Color Is Your Parachute? A Practical Manual for Job-Hunters and Career-Changers* (2002 edition), by Richard Nelson

Bolles. It's an excellent book to guide you through the career-changing or job-hunting process.

- Discover a new passion by taking an evening or weekend class in something that you've always found fascinating.
- Follow the personal and career paths that are fulfilling to you. Don't let anyone disturb your groove.
- Stop procrastinating. Tomorrow is not promised.
- Grow your own crop of hope. You may start out bad at something, then you practice, then you get better. Watch yourself soar with each new day.

57. Do your fair share.

Doing nothing is doing evil.

—Proverb

Sure, it's a lot easier and less taxing to sit back and watch those around us do all the work. Your inner voice, though, always reminds you that you know better—even if you don't do what it says.

Rather than always rushing to get your part over with, take pride in assigned tasks, approach them with care, stay focused, and put your best foot forward every time. That way, when your labor is complete, you may reward yourself for a job well done.

When we do our fair share of the household chores, the monthly report, or the grunt work on a community project, we feel better about ourselves, as though we contributed something. When we do our part, we can humbly say, "Look what I've done" with a clear conscience and pride.

Being a team player goes beyond the football field and the office. We must assert that same lively spirit at home with our families and significant others. We must put forth as much effort in doing our fair share of playing with the pets, assisting our children with their homework, working in the yard, and grocery shopping as we do contributing to the boss's monthly report and scoring a touchdown for the team.

Roll up your sleeves and pitch in!

Action Steps

- Share responsibility at home. Call a family meeting to discuss who will do which chores around the house. Then make up a schedule for what will be done and when. Post the schedule in a place for all to see.

- Tithe at church.

- Participate in your neighborhood homeowners' association.

- Share diaper-changing duties—it's your baby, too.

- Give your mate a break—*you* give the kids their nightly baths, read them their bedtime stories, and lay out their school clothes this week.

58. Check your social wellness.

The key to success is to keep growing in all areas of your life—mental, emotional, spiritual, as well as physical.

—Julius "Dr. J." Irving, athlete

For the black man, wellness for the mind, body, and spirit is critical. Health experts define wellness as an active process through which an individual becomes aware of and makes choices toward a more successful existence.

There are six diverse dimensions of wellness that make us whole: emotional, intellectual, career/occupational, spiritual, physical, and social. Let's focus here on social wellness, since many men, particularly African-American men, don't take time to take stock of their own state of social well-being.

Straight up—a brother is merely a reflection of his physical, mental, and social well-being. To be healthy means more than just being physically fit and disease-free. It also means focusing on developing and enhancing positive life choices that enable us to sustain the highest possible levels of our total selves. As we travel through life, we encounter stress, challenges, and difficulties. However, by adopting a socially well lifestyle, we can better prepare and enable ourselves to deal with these hurdles and to make the most of what life offers. When we live in this way, we actively choose to invite optimism, resilience, and other life-enhancing elements into the very whole of our lives.

One of the greatest parts about living a socially well lifestyle is that even difficulties are easier to champion, which is particularly important for us as men of color. Remember, to foster ourselves as healthy individuals is to foster a healthy African-American community, from which the rewards to all are great.

Here are a few affirmations related to social wellness. How many of them can you affirm for yourself?

My life is in my hands, and I control it.

I am an active member of one or more community organizations (e.g., black-male mentoring, church choir, antiviolence, AIDS awareness, or environmental-preservation).

I am satisfied with my ability to relax.

I enjoy my own company and relish being alone sometimes.

I allow myself to experience a full range of emotions—fear, sadness, anger, and joy—and I find constructive ways to express them without any hangups.

I am able to sleep at night because I am at peace with
myself.

I am able to stand in front of a full-length mirror,
looking at myself from head to toe, knowing that I
accept my outer appearance.

I feel okay about crying alone or in the presence of
other men and women—and allow myself to do so.

I am able to initiate a conversation with others.

I approach life with the attitude that no problem is too
big to solve.

Action Steps

- If you're unable to apply the above affirmations to your daily
life, you may need do some self-reconstruction. Start your
journey right now.

- Recognize your need for leisure and make time for fun constructive projects, dating, and other recreational activities.

- Develop, cultivate, and value deep friendships with both men
and women.

- Learn to exhibit comfort and ease in a variety of situations
during work and play.

- Be aware of societal changes and cultural diversity, and adjust archaic attitudes appropriately.

- Learn to interact well with and appreciate the differences in
people of both sexes, different backgrounds, lifestyles, ethnic-
ities, and ages.

- Visit your local bookstore or library to read and learn more
about the six dimensions of wellness.

59. Live your wildest dream!

If you can learn to think big, nothing on earth will keep
you from being successful in whatever you choose to do.

—Dr. Benjamin Carson, director of pediatric neurosurgery,
Johns Hopkins Hospital

With all the books today urging us to "dream big," you would think we'd get a clue and do it.

Too often we sit idly by and watch others fulfill their dreams. We think "Hmm . . . must be nice," and keep on living the routine life to which we desperately wish to add spice.

If you want something, go after it. Make your plan, set your focus, and take action! Think big! This usually means stepping outside your comfort zone, taking what others may call unthinkable risks. If you can believe it, you really can achieve it. What a feeling it is to tell yourself, "You just lived your wildest dream!"

The alternative is a scenario like the one involving Robert, a photographer for a daily newspaper. Every time he's covering an assignment in a wealthy neighborhood, he sighs. "I'll never live in a home like that," he says, pointing to a million-dollar mansion surrounded by rolling hills. Robert, his wife, and three kids live in an upper-middle-class black neighborhood. They live pretty well; both he and his wife work hard to maintain what they have.

Robert's mistake is he actually could have that million-dollar mansion if he really wants it. Each time he passes by and says "I'll never have that," he is reinforcing negative energy against the idea that he could have it.

If we never dream big, never think big, we will never have anything big. What if Robert chose, instead, to say, "I'm going to have that one day," or, "I'm working toward getting a home like that." Nothing is wrong with that.

When we focus our attention on and set our minds to something we want, we begin to visualize the possibility of it happening. So if you want the big house, think about ways to go about getting it. If you want to send your daughter to Harvard, start thinking about ways to get her there. If you want your boy to go to Morehouse College, start now plotting the course that will enable you to help pay the tuition.

Realize that if you never initiate the thought process, that big thing will never ever happen. Know that if you don't think big, don't expect to live your wildest dream.

Action Steps

- Take five minutes to think about the unimaginable—something super-positive that would give you such a high you would find it hard to believe.
- Never suppress your own wants and desires to satisfy others. Not friends. Not parents. Not mentors. Not siblings. Don't do it!
- Share your "wildest dream" with your partner. Perhaps you'll garner some help in making it come true sooner than you thought.
- Never fear dreaming big.
- Start being positive when thinking about what you want.
- Remember that anything worth having will take hard work to get.
- Review homes in for-sale booklets to help you decide what you want in your dream house.

60. Be independent.

Being your own man does not mean taking advantage of anyone else.

—Flip Wilson, entertainer

Clarence Jr. was one of seven children born to Mabel and her late husband. He's a sixty-two-year-old single man who's always relied on the kindness of the women in his life to help him do the everyday things that most folks should be able to do for themselves—cooking, ironing, sewing on shirt buttons, and spending money responsibly. After all, now that he and his second wife Clara have finally called it quits, he knew Mama would always make sure her youngest son got everything he needed: cab fare, his favorite foods, and a car he could drive (once he decided to get his driver's license). Following his divorce, Clarence Jr. moved in with Mama. There he got to live rent-free. Mama was just glad to have another man about the house for her own safety. For three years she delighted in the company, until her own sudden death.

It's been a week now since Mama passed away, and Clarence Jr. lives alone in the big empty house with clothes he can't wash, a refrigerator stocked with food he can't cook, and an oven he couldn't clean with Easy-Off if his life depended on it.

For most of his adult life, Clarence Jr. relied on one too many ladyfriends, "good ol' Mama," and an attentive sister and aunt who always made sure he had at least two things: a pot of beef stew (since that was something he could stretch out all week), and freshly starched shirts at the top of each week.

Now at an impasse, Clarence Jr. struggles daily to perform simple tasks that every man should be able to do. His daily routine consists of picking up fast food and staring at the mountains of dirty clothes stuffed in a closet and the piles of dirty dishes in the kitchen that have been there since Mama died.

As infants and children, we had no choice but to rely on parents and caregivers to do for us what we could not do or did not know how to do for ourselves. As we grew older, we were given more to do. Cleaning our own rooms. Picking up items at the grocery store. Washing the dinner dishes. These were chores that taught us responsibility.

Women's work? Hardly, man. Whether married with children or single and living alone—or with your own "Mama Mabel"—as adult men, we need to know how to do more than take out the trash, run the vacuum, make bacon-and-egg sandwiches, and know what clothes to wash together and separately. We should know how to follow a recipe for a favorite meat loaf as well as we can follow the instruction manual for a new CD-changer.

It's time for the manchild like Clarence Jr. to get busy and start doing the things he should have been doing years ago.

Are you a Clarence Jr.?

Action Steps

- Instill in your children—especially sons—the knowledge of how to cook, clean house, sew, and shop for groceries. Learning early on teaches them responsibility and how to be self-reliant.

- If you don't know how to wash which clothes with what, ask someone who knows how to do laundry to teach you. You really need to know.

- Clean your house on a weekly basis, gentlemen. It keeps dust from piling up, food from molding in the fridge, and the glass-top table from becoming a gooey mess.

- Realize that no one should have to pick up your socks or dirty underwear off the floor or scrub your signature ring from around the tub. Neither your mate nor your mama is your maid, so don't treat them that way.

- Stop sending your shirts out for commercial laundering every week. Not only will you spend a fortune every month, you'll ultimately damage the shirts. Wash and iron them yourself, at least during alternate weeks.

61. Be affectionate.

Make some muscle in your head but use the muscle in your heart.

—Imamu Amiri Baraka, author

Why is it so hard for a man to show affection? This is an age-old question women have pondered for centuries. After all, it seems women can express what's on *their* minds with a single caress of our brow, a gentle squeeze of our finger, or spontaneous head-rest on our shoulder. Maybe up there on Venus they're taught that showing affection is actually quite the human thing to do. Meanwhile, on Mars we are told it is "unmanly" to do so.

Not until recent years did we finally get it—it's cool to tell Pops "I love you, man," hug another man other than the coach, or cuddle with Gina just after lovemaking.

Perhaps in your old man's day, men didn't show such an emotional side of themselves. Overall, men have come a long way in the showing of emotions, and today your pops might just appreciate that hug more than you know. A simple "Hey, baby, how was your day?" to your mate; a loving good-bye kiss to your sons; or a sincere compliment to the boss can warm a heart, affirm a soul, and nurture a spirit. Those are feelings in which we all take pleasure—no matter what planet we're from.

Action Steps

- Hug your son(s) and daughter(s) three times today—just because they're special, and they're yours.

- Rub or grease your partner's scalp tonight just before bed—like folks used to do.

- Give your mate a foot massage tonight. Do it while the two of you are watching your favorite TV show or while your mate is reading a favorite book.

- Show affection toward your mate in front of your children. Witnessing parents' love and affection for each other can make children feel warm inside as well, and it gives them a strong sense of what commitment means.

- Tonight, take a hot bubble bath with your wife. Surround the tub with burning candles. Play the romantic and soothing *This Is My Beloved* CD, by brother Arthur Prysock in the background. Have warm towels waiting nearby for drying each other off.

- Don't be shy about showing *yourself* some love by self-pampering. Draw and indulge in your own soothing bath a few times this week. Brothers need to get into their solitude too.

62. Live in the spirit of the Million Man March.

Long live the spirit of the Million Man March!
—chant spoken during the historic Million Man March

One million strong!

What else can be said about the historic march on Washington in October of 1995? A lot.

It is not so much that we went, talked, and listened. What is paramount is what we do back in our own communities with all of that knowledge we gained.

The spirit of the historic march was about brotherhood. We heard about collective work and responsibility; how to start taking responsibility for our own actions; learning why it's important to vote and be active; why we should spend our dollars in our neighborhoods first. If we are to keep the spirit of the march alive, we must rekindle the fire of enthusiasm each and every day at home, at work, and at school. Our very existence may well depend on how well we live in the spirit of the Million Man March.

Imagine that scene one more time: One million brothers from every corner of the country, from different socioeconomic backgrounds, from different neighborhoods, with different opinions, but with a common goal—unity.

Now imagine what can be done if that energy, that spirit, is allowed to bloom and grow throughout America. Imagine if those one million black men each get five people to register to vote, get five people to vote on election day, get five people to shop regularly at a black bookstore, get five people to invest in a black bank, get five people to have annual health checkups.

Just imagine . . .

Action Steps

- Invest in your community. Whether your money or your time, whatever you put in, you are likely to get double back.

- Tell a friend who didn't attend about the Million Man March. If you don't share what you know about the lessons learned, the good vibes will never be passed on.

- Contact your relatives and friends and ask them if they're still living in the spirit of the march. If they're not or have forgotten about October 1995, make it your business to remind them.

- Do one thing today to lift up yourself.

63. Have a hobby.

Blessed are those who can please themselves.

—Zulu proverb

Remember your rock collection? Marbles? Hot Wheels? Your Lionel train set? Your old 8mm home-movie collection? Your stamp collection? What about that comic-book collection stored in your parents' attic?

Our lives change constantly, sometimes requiring us to put our hobbies on hold while raising our children, returning to school, or starting a new career. We're often reminded of our interests of old through the smell of old manuals and the feel of old gadgets while cleaning out closets, old footlockers, or the garage. Those kind of discoveries can flood the mind with memories, even leave us feeling wistful. They were fascinating activities we enjoyed in younger days with less pressures. However, occasionally reflecting on old hobbies isn't always enough. Picking them up again later in life can rejuvenate old passions and inspire creative energy. And you thought those days were gone? Wrong.

While you're busy doing for others, be sure to take time out for yourself to resurrect old pleasures. Doing so can take the edge off even the roughest day at home or on the job.

Perhaps as a younger man you enjoyed collecting baseball cards or action figures. Dig them up—they might even be worth a fortune by now. Did you enjoy days of fishing with Granddaddy? Then pull out the old rod and the reel he left to you; he'd be proud. What about those model cars you used to build? After all these years, can't you still smell the model glue? Don't just savor the sights and smells of yesteryear. Spark your old passions. While you're at it, take time to discover new ones along the way.

Action Steps

- Take up an old hobby or develop a new one such as computing, or collecting works of art by your favorite sculptor or painter.
- Share your interests with friends and family members.
- If you're a computer buff, join the computer-users group in your area. If you're a former "Trekkie," attend the next *Star Trek* convention or trade show that comes to town.
- Take a class in something you've always thought would be cool to learn to do, like painting, photography, gardening, or snorkeling. You name it, just do it!

64. Discover your sexual self.

It's your thing.

—Isley Brothers, entertainers

Determining what you like, how you like it, and who you like it with requires some sexual self-discovery. As you may know, all the answers can't be found inside the pages of the newest sex manual, in nude photographs of glossy magazines, or in steamy videos (even though they're all famous for the self-pleasures they inspire).

To know what brings you true pleasure under the covers is to look at your past and current life to see what patterns have defined your sexuality through the years. If you like a good mystery, you will enjoy discovering clues to your sexual identity.

Today's man is gradually learning to connect his emotions with the idea of good sex. We can distinguish between a quick romp in the sack and gripping lovemaking. Fortunately the current AIDS crisis, in both the heterosexual, bisexual, and homosexual communities, coupled with the startling number of children with absentee fathers, have forced men young and old to begin to re-examine their attitudes toward their partners, their bodies, their wants, and their desires.

Sex and health experts tell us, in fact, that the art of solo sex is good for us emotionally and physically. Those private moments can provide opportunities for exploring our own bodies and discovering what brings us the most pleasure. Every intelligent and sensible brother knows that if he indulges in sexual self-gratification he won't be struck blind or insane, banished to hell, or fall victim to any of the other tragedies those ridiculous old wives' tales had black folk believing at one time.

Brothermen, when we're honest with ourselves and aware of our own erogenous zones, we can effectively communicate those new finds to our partners the next time we share intimate moments together. Ask your "main squeeze" to rub your temples, gently bite your earlobes, or suck your toes during passionate lovemaking. Or maybe tell her to "talk dirty" to you during the throes of passion.

It's time we acknowledge it's okay to discover our sexual selves. Start your journey in the shower, in the kitchen, or wherever you most enjoy doin a little "sumthin' sumthin' "—with or without your partner.

Action Steps

- Encourage solo sex in your partner relationship. Stop keeping what you might consider a "dirty little secret" from your mate.

- Tonight, show your wife or partner how and where to put her hands on you.

- Know that while masturbating is not sinful but part of human nature, as with anything, obsession is not emotionally or physically healthy.

- Produce a list of all the sex partners you've been with through the years. List as many as you can. Which encounters gave you the most satisfaction? Did any put you at any health risk?

- Take a few moments to think about which sexual acts you find the most appealing and those at which you seem to be most adept.

- Give some thought to the type of person to whom you are consistently drawn.

- Think about the fantasy that you've longed to try but haven't for one reason or another.

- Ask yourself if there were any times that you found yourself succumbing to sexual pressure. If so, determine whether you're strong enough not to succumb again.

65. Play more than basketball and football.

Baseball is a far better sport than football; the pay is better, the longevity is better, and the pension plan is better. But for some reason, black players seem to gravitate towards sports [like basketball and football] that allow them to emphasize the showtime factor.

—A. S. "Doc" Young, sports journalist and author

Many of us have a favorite sport. Some like tennis, some golf, others racquetball, but many of us like basketball and football. This is fine, but we must find ways to explore the other sports of the world that African Americans can play and excel in.

What if there were no Tiger Woods or Calvin Peete? What if Venus and Serena Williams and Arthur Ashe had never picked up a tennis racquet? What if Pelé never used his feet to soar to new heights? What if Wendell Scott never got behind the wheel? What if Jair Lynch never bothered to enter a gym and take on the parallel bars? What if there had never been a Jackie Robinson? You get the point.

For sure, the above sports have long been enjoyed by African Americans, but they haven't gotten anywhere near as much attention as we pay to the sports of Michael "Air" Jordan, or Deion "Primetime" Sanders.

We should make a valiant effort now to expand the horizons of our young people in as many sports as possible. We should even tackle sports like polo or croquet when given the chance. How about archery? Why not swimming? If for no other reason, we should make sure we do this because far more business deals are cut on the greens and the tennis courts than on the basketball court or gridiron.

Action Steps

- Learn to play golf. You will find chasing after a little white ball isn't as bad as it looks.

- Take your son or daughter to a tennis court at a young age to start them learning early. If your child enjoys the sport, you could have a future Wimbledon champion on your hands.

- Attend the Olympic Games if you ever get a chance. Just seeing the different sports in action may inspire you to give some new ones a try.

- Play more than one sport, and if they're basketball and football, play more than two.

- Read a monthly magazine about sports or regularly visit a sports Web site. You may be surprised by the wealth of information you can glean from a magazine or the Internet. You may also find there are many others who are interested in a sport but don't have friends to participate with. You can meet new friends while learning a new sport.

66. Be prepared.

It's better to look ahead and prepare than to look back and regret.
—Jackie Joyner-Kersee, Olympic champion

Every good Boy Scout learns to always be prepared. You don't, however, have to don a uniform to adhere to this timeless piece of advice. Of course, we can't anticipate everything that pops up in our lives; it's unrealistic to think we could. However, we sure can equip ourselves with what we need to ward off many disastrous occurrences. In battle, good soldiers arm themselves with the weapons they need to protect themselves. Good sportsmen follow a good playbook and map out strategy. A serious and dedicated musician rehearses many hours to perform his very best. Let's take a lesson from them to keep ourselves prepared for what has the potential to come our way, too.

Action Steps

- Back up your computer hard drive once a week. One major system crash, and those files could be gone forever.

- Save copies of significant and confidential files on a separate CD or zip disk, and store it in a safe place—in case the computer is stolen.

- Keep a change of clothes, a set of tools, and a blanket in the trunk of your car, truck, or van. You never know when overnight stays or emergencies will pop up.

- Use computer software that allows you to input a database and description of all the items in your home. In the event of theft or damage, you'll be thankful for your good documentation.

- Keep a written record of all birthdays, anniversaries, and other special dates. You'll land in the doghouse if you forget.

- Make sure your personal organizer or calendar is always with you.

- Make a photocopied sheet that contains the front and back of all your credit, insurance, and membership cards and the other contents of your wallet. If your wallet is lost or stolen, you'll have a record of exactly what was in it.

- Keep paper and pen with you at all times.

- Always have thirty-five cents on you. You never know when you'll need to make a phone call.

- If you're sexually active, keep condoms near your bedside (never, ever in your wallet). You'll be glad you did when in the heat of the moment, you won't find yourself having to make a trek to the bathroom to retrieve them—an instant mood-changer!

- Keep a rainy-day fund. Money on reserve can be a lifesaver.

- Keep your cell phone and pager batteries charged at all times.

- Keep a spare check hidden in your car. There's nothing like being in line at the store and discovering your checkbook is empty!

- Keep a spare car key in your wallet. You'll be thankful if you ever lock yourself out.

- Forgot to mail that card in time? Don't worry—zap the person an *on-line* birthday, congratulations, or Kwanzaa greeting via the Internet. Your communiqué will arrive instantly!

67. Schedule daily "me time."

Solitude, quality solitude, is an assertion of self-worth, because only in the stillness can we hear the truth of our unique voices.

—Pearl Cleage, playwright and author

Have you ever felt like it was all just too much? Most of us have at one time or another. The kids' Little League game is tonight, and it's your week to carpool. Your wife forgot to pay the bill, and now the phone's been disconnected. The dog has yet to be fed, walked, and played with, so he's goin' nuts! You've promised to take Uncle James to look for a new suit this weekend—and you know that's an experience in itself. Sixteen voice-mail messages await—let alone the ones back at the office. The rash on your arm has reared its ugly head again. Now, the *&@! computer keeps crashing—and that report is due when?

Whew! Everybody needs a little time away—as the song by the group Chicago goes. In today's fast-paced world, those lyrics couldn't have more meaning.

As our personal daily rounds seem more and more compli-cated, our heads get filled with more noise than ever before. Well, sooner or later something's got to give, or else—it can make a man feel he's going to "lose it" if he doesn't rein it all in.

Working your fingers to the bone without downtime can lead to an assortment of problems affecting your physical and mental health and even relationships with your family and friends who may or may not be on the merry-go-round with you.

Mastering the skills of good time management to get it all done is fine. However, just be sure to include somewhere in your best-laid plans that all-important time with yourself. Commence your daily "me time" today. Pick a place that's away from the noise. Maybe your time is 4 A.M., before every-one else gets up. It could be late at night, after everyone else is fast asleep. Whatever works for you. After the first few times alone, you will discover that this newfound solitude can even introduce you to sides of yourself you may have not known existed.

Family members may not always understand. Friends may

accuse you of acting funny. Coworkers may say you're isolating yourself. No matter. Simply explain to them why your personal downtime is important to you—to eradicate the stress, enable you to center yourself, or make you more pleasant to be around. If they fail to understand, not a problem. They will work through it, with or without your help.

Personal time to reflect, work, enjoy peace and quiet, or simply get centered is a vital part of life.

Action Steps

- When staying in for lunch at work, eat in peace by hanging a MEETING IN PROGRESS—DO NOT DISTURB sign on your office door; then forward your phone to voice mail and turn off your pager.
- Next week, begin getting up at least an hour earlier, before everyone else in the house does.
- Create your own island of tranquility in the house where you can retreat for your "me time." Fill it with your favorite easy chair, CDs, spiritual books, and videos.
- Pick out a serene spot in the park that's ideal for meditating or praying.
- Consider something radical: Take a marriage sabbatical. A break from your mate. A week or two of solitude and self-centering in the mountains or at your family's or friends' time-share may give you the space you need to assess and reorder your life. Your positive transformation could ultimately improve your marriage and relationship with your children.
- Sometimes, just take time out to do absolutely *nothing*—just be.

68. Recognize your *own* prejudices before calling others on theirs.

Racism, sexism, anti-Semitism, ableism, and homophobia are learned! So we can unlearn them. Better yet, we could just stop teaching them.
—Johnnetta B. Cole, former president of Spelman College

They say folks in glass houses shouldn't throw stones. We're so quick to point out the prejudicial or racist behaviors of others. Yet when it comes to our own behavior, African Americans' acceptance track record isn't exactly squeaky clean. Some are content to make like the ostrich, burying their heads in the sandbox of ignorance, fear, and denial.

We're afraid to touch someone if she's gay. We're hesitant to trust someone if he's white or is of the Buddhist faith. And, Lord, help us, because we're scared to death to embrace or comfort someone with AIDS, cancer, mental illness, or is physically challenged. Maybe we think who they are or what they have will somehow rub off on us, making us "one of *those* people."

What many of us don't realize is that the same fear that some whites had (and some still have) of "the Nigras" is driven by the same ignorance that compels some black folks to shun even one of our own.

Bisexuality and homosexuality. They are lifestyles that have always existed in our community, but have been considered too taboo to acknowledge and address without fear. In fact, some brothers can't fix their mouths to even say the words much less befriend a brother or sister who is gay or bisexual. Rather, guys thrive on name-calling, throwing around words like "sissy," "dyke," "faggot," or "shaky." Some men and women who lead an "alternative lifestyle" are simply written off and acknowledged as "that's just Damon," or "Girl, you know about Joellen, right?"

How about religion? If theirs is different from ours, "it's got to be the work of the devil." Many adults can recall the days when, as children, they would watch Saturday morning cartoons while Mama would fix breakfast. When that all-too-familiar knock on the door sounded, with one swift movement Mama would snatch the children up and throw them behind the couch with the execution of a ninja, as she whispered, "Shh . . . Don't move. It's those Jehovah's Witness folks. We ain't home."

What of "cracker," "white boy," and "redneck?" These are just a few of the derogatory terms black folks have used to describe whites. While some black Americans have found it in their hearts to forgive, we haven't forgotten the turbulent history of abuse at the hands of white America. It's now time to examine our own racist and discriminatory actions toward the white race. We must move on.

Ingrained anger and self-interpreted Bible scripture can conveniently justify our dislike or hatred for individuals whom we view as different from ourselves. However, not until we commit ourselves to opening our minds, educate ourselves, and respect differences in our fellow men will we eradicate ignorance based on our fears and phobias. We've asked this of others. Now it's time to apply it to ourselves.

As black men, most of us know plenty about being on the bottom rung of the American social ladder. So, to condemn and lash out at others for the lives they lead, the faiths they follow, the skin color they bear is to keep alive the hatred, the stereotypes, the degradation people have worked so hard for centuries to erase.

You may not agree with others' beliefs and ways of life, but always embrace and respect differences. As positive, strong brothers we have the power to cultivate change in ourselves and in the black community. Let's start adjusting our attitudes.

Action Steps

- Take five minutes right now to think about your own attitudes toward people of another race, lifestyle, or religion. Jot down your thoughts, and think about the similarities or differences between your attitudes and the attitudes of those who have oppressed African Americans throughout the years.

- Work to increase your tolerance of others you know who are different from you.

- Make a conscious effort daily to refrain from passing on racist thinking patterns and actions to your children.

- Rather than shying away from someone who may be different from you, talk with him or her to discover your similar interests and commonalities.

69. Discover the creative you.

Create, and be true to yourself, and depend only on your own good taste.
—Duke Ellington, composer and entertainer

Most times when we describe someone as being "gifted" or "very creative," thoughts of great works of art, literature, or musical masterpieces come to mind. However, great creative talents aren't limited to our ancient Egyptian ancestors, Langston Hughes, Walter Mosley, or Scott Joplin.

All of us are blessed with creative talents, whether for building computers, writing poetry, composing rap music, or baking a rum cake "that'll make you slap your mama!" However, it's discovering what we're good at that can be a bit of a challenge. Some men discover their creative side at an early age. Others reach their senior years before creativity finally breaks through. Yet most of us will go to our graves never knowing how many talents lay dormant while we were alive.

But that doesn't have to be your fate, bro. Do something this week to help tap the potentially rich talents within. Something as simple as taking a class in auto mechanics, a foreign language, or singing at the community college can open up your talents!

Action Steps

- Test out the old vocal cords in the shower next time no one's around to hear you. Sing to your heart's content loud and strong! The shampoo bottle's a great makeshift microphone. There could be a Johnny Mathis, Nat "King" Cole, or Brian McKnight just itching to get out!

- If you can paint a mean house, try your hand at painting on canvas. Or stop by the hobby shop and pick up a paint-by-numbers set—like the one you had as a kid.

- Share your new or current hobby with others—your girl-friend, a cousin, your poker buddies, or golf partner.

70. Know what motivates you.

It's been said that no one can really motivate anyone else; all you can do is instill a positive attitude and hope it catches on.

—Eddie Robinson, former football coach
of Grambling State University

What gets you pumped, brother? Really pumped? So much so that you feel you can conquer the world?

Perhaps it's a bonus at work. A perfect score on an exam. Reverend Thomas's lively Sunday-morning service. Or how about brother Les Brown's or sister Iyanla Vanzant's knock-

'em-dead words of inspiration and affirmation. Or does it simply take a swift kick in the butt for you to get moving? That's all right, too, because, some of us need hotter fires under us than others.

Knowing what truly motivates us is our key to reaching personal and professional goals, staying healthy, or keeping the word we give to others. Without motivation, we can wander aimlessly throughout our lives, never knowing what heights we're able to reach, what dreams we can attain, and what mountains we can move.

There will always be valleys to cross, obstacles to overcome. However, if we're armed with self-motivation, there's nothing we can't do. Let's get pumped!

Action Steps

- Check out the assortment of motivational audio books at your favorite bookstore. There are tons of titles featuring your favorite authors and speakers.

- Pull out that piece of paper on which you wrote down your New Year's resolutions. Gauge how far you've come or how far away you are from making those resolutions realities.

- When beginning a new exercise routine, have a friend or a mate get with the program with you. You can keep each other motivated to stick with the plan for a healthier lifestyle for yourselves.

- Determine your strengths and weaknesses and put the information to work for you.

- Help to motivate someone else. Today, share an inspirational word with a sister or brother who's feeling hopeless or distraught. Your words just might be the spark they need to make changes they thought might never be possible.

71. Enlighten yourself.

*The man who views the world at fifty the same as he did
when he was twenty has wasted thirty years of his life.*
—Muhammad Ali, humanitarian and former
heavyweight boxing champion

At its core, to enlighten is to provide information, to inform or instruct, to become aware. We need to realize that there is so much out there for us to see, to learn, and to enjoy.

When Bryant Gumbel persuaded NBC to go to Africa to air a series of reports, it enlightened many of us about the Motherland. When we read the works of writer Ernest Gaines, we are enlightened about our heritage. When we take a trip to the cotton fields in the South, we are enlightened by the lessons we learn about our forefathers' and foremothers' struggle for freedom.

As the twenty-first century begins, black men have access to more information than ever. There are no excuses.

John Johnson didn't have the Internet when he started his publishing empire. University libraries weren't always open to blacks when Langston Hughes wrote his literary works. Black folks didn't have voter information when Adam Clayton Powell and Charles Diggs went to Washington to fight for our rights on Capitol Hill.

Enough said. Enlighten yourself, brothers. All the tools you need are before you, and most are free of charge. So start cashing in, now! Taking just one of the Action Steps below this week will start you well on your way.

Action Steps

- Have a conversation with your grandfather. Ask him about his childhood or his days in the service.
- Pick up a book on world religions at the bookstore.

- Read the back of the cereal box and milk carton this morning to see exactly what you're consuming.
- Drop in on your children's school for a half day of observation.
- Read the comics in the Sunday paper.
- Watch public television tonight rather than the network news or your favorite sitcom.
- Clean out your attic.
- Watch *Jeopardy!*
- Review your insurance policy with your agent.
- Take part in the conversation at the barbershop.
- Cruise the Internet. And while you're logged on, visit http://www.askmen.com (Cool Web site!)

72. Do something "just because."

Kindness is never wasted. If it has no effect on the recipient, at least it benefits the bestower.

—Unknown

When was the last time you did something "just because" or for yourself or for someone else?

Sometimes we get so caught up in our daily routines and responsibilities on the job, in the classroom, or with outside activities, we forget to bestow upon our loved ones and ourselves those random acts of kindness that can renew the body, mind, and spirit. Even if the "little somethings" you do produce nothing more than a smile, your efforts are worthwhile.

It's been said that there's a reason for everything, and why we act and do the things we do. The reasons are many and varied. Remember, that long list of reasons includes "just because I wanted to." Let us always treasure the "little things" and random acts of kindness life brings our way.

Action Steps

- Today, call a gift shop that delivers and surprise your mate with flowers or a balloon bouquet "just because."
- Buy two ball game tickets for yourself and a buddy to see your favorite team play.
- Write and mail your special someone a love letter. Think of the smile you will bring to that face you love as the letter is being read.
- This week, take time out to call two family members—one you have not talked to in ages, and one you talk to frequently—just to tell him or her: "I was just thinking about you" and "I love you."
- Take out the trash without being asked.
- Next time you stop at a traffic light and decide to help someone standing on the corner holding a sign that reads HUNGRY. PLEASE HELP, rather than giving a buck, *feed* the person. Try giving him or her a sandwich, easily picked up at a nearby fast-food drive-thru. You will know exactly where your dollar went.
- Give your wife a handmade coupon good for one shopping trip together without complaints.

73. Don't let it take a tragedy to turn your life around.

In every crisis there is a message. Crises are nature's way of forcing change—breaking down old structures, shaking loose negative habits so that something new and better can take their place.

—Susan Taylor, editor in chief of *Essence* magazine and author

Siblings Willie and Overton had a tough childhood. Unfortunately Willie's jealousy of Overton plagued their relationship until tragedy struck.

One night, in one of his infamous drunken rages, Willie showed up on Overton's doorstep. He was talking the same old trash about how Overton always thought he was so much better, that he and his family flaunted their money with their new home and two luxury cars, and how "Mama and Daddy loved you more than me."

After forcing his way inside the house, Willie, armed with his "piece," began threatening to take his brother out and shut him up once and for all. In a two-minute struggle to grab the gun, two bullets emptied into Overton's forehead and abdomen, killing him instantly.

Overton's wife, Verna, and young daughter, Angela, stood in shock as Willie hovered over his brother's body lying in a pool of blood.

Willie was arrested for his crime. He now serves a prison sentence for the murder of his only brother. Although he's been sober for three years and has undergone counseling for his personal insecurities, what he did may haunt him for the rest of his life. Sure, he's cleaned up his act. He even talks with young brothers about going straight. Every day, though, he struggles to forgive himself for pulling the trigger. As for his sister-in-law and niece, they continue to get through another day without Overton, a loving husband and father who risked his own life to save theirs, and to save his brother from himself.

Stories like this one unfold every day within our own communities. We hear them on the news. We read them in the newspaper. Some brothers we know have been part of tragic dramas like this one.

Tragedy shouldn't have to strike before you turn your life around. However, most of us don't begin to work on ourselves until life begins to fall apart. Remember, change is usually sparked by two catalysts—desperation or inspiration. If you have a choice, opt for the latter—its rewards are sweet!

Are you struggling with tough personal issues right now? Is envy, hatred, or sadness eating away at you right now? Get help somewhere, man, before you do something you, too, could regret for the rest of your life.

Action Steps

- Get some counseling or therapy if you feel you're anywhere close to where Willie was in dealing with a family or friend or foe.

- Stop, and go for a walk if you're in an argument that's heating up.

- Help a friend get some help if you know he is on a warpath like Willie's. Sometimes you have to be your friend's conscience when his gets out of whack.

- Realize that although you may not be able to *forget* something bad you did to someone else, you must be willing to *forgive* yourself before old wounds can heal.

74. Respect your environment.

It looks like the devil had a fit in here!

—African-American saying

The environments in which we live, work, and play should be held sacred. When we have regard for our environment, we show respect for ourselves.

When we keep our lawns well tended, the rooms in our home clean, and our desks at work tidy, we give off a sense of having order about ourselves. Just because some of us may be considered disadvantaged and live in public housing, it doesn't mean we have to let our neighborhoods look run-down. Just because we may not have the income to furnish and live in the homes we may desire doesn't mean we can't keep a clean and healthy home where we do live. Just because our day at the workplace is "helter skelter," we need not be disheveled and carefree with our work space.

To recite that old adage: "Cleanliness is next to godliness."

Action Steps

- Don't litter.
- Keep up your property.
- If you can't afford cleaning materials, contact a local nonprofit organization for assistance.
- Keep your car tuned up to prevent excess emissions from polluting the air.
- Respect the property of others and the environment.
- Don't smoke in areas where others may object; if you haven't quit yet, find a place where you don't infringe on their rights to safe and clean air.
- If you see someone littering, advise him it's not a good idea.

75. Brother, humble thyself!

A person completely wrapped up in himself makes a small package.

—Denzel Washington, entertainer

Are you the man? Think so, huh? Well, we all like to feel important and get pats on the back for a job well done at home or at the office. Everyone likes—and even deserves—to have their praises sung every now and then. It's part of human nature.

As men of color, we might feel the need to assert ourselves a little more than our white male counterparts—just to materialize from the invisible state we sometimes live in. While we struggle to be acknowledged—and at least be seen in the boardroom and in the classroom—we have to be careful not to unconsciously kick into overdrive to prove our expertise, authority, and confidence. This kind of behavior makes those with whom we interact label us abrasive, unapproachable, or too full of ourselves. You can be confident without being arrogant.

So, the next time you start gettin' all "biggety," as Big Mama says, have Mr. Ego check his attitude at the door and take it with him when he leaves. Affirming ourselves for the vast knowledge we possess can be done with tact and finesse when we interact with others. Remember, true self-confidence stands on its own merit.

Action Steps

- Read the Bible; it is filled with stories that will teach you humility.

- Offer to help somebody who works under you, or is in a position of lesser influence. It's likely someone helped you on your way up.

- Stop criticizing others' successes; use them as a way to inspire you to move to the next level in your work or endeavors.

- Be humble now; don't wait until tomorrow.

76. Have a sense of humor.

Laughing stirs up the blood, expands the chest, electrifies the nerves, clears away the cobwebs from the brain, and gives the whole system a cleansing rehabilitation.

—Unknown

It can bend you double. It can make you cry. It's even been known to help heal the sick. To be such an ordinary expression, laughter sure possesses a lot of power. Just ask someone who makes others laugh for a living.

Laughter has been a soothing balm to the black soul for centuries. Since being brought to these shores from our native land, our quick wit and sense of humor helped keep us sane. Granted, there were times when there was very little to laugh about; however, the ability to spread good humor has been a source of our strength. Our ability to entertain ourselves and others has helped us over the hurdles of pain and suffering we've encountered. Even through the most difficult times we can laugh at ourselves.

Black folks will crack you up with wide-ranging jokes and witticisms about black life and our Caucasian counterparts' perceptions about black people. Get us together in a room, and we'll make you split your sides. Crackin' on each other. Talkin' 'bout who's doin' what to whom at work and at church.

Sure, most of us don't have the comedic and hit-home genius of Chris Rock and Jackie "Moms" Mabley, or the spontaneity and raw humor of J. Anthony Brown or Whoopi

Goldberg. Yet even we lesser humorists have the talent to make each other laugh 'til we cry.

Whether you're a whooper or a hollerer, a good laugh can make you forget a current crisis or the cause of a heavy heart and even lighten the load of the heaviest grief. One of the best things about having a sense of humor is that you can still get tickled years later, long after the laughter has stopped ringing. So, go on and laugh. It's good for you.

Action Steps

- Take in some comedy tonight. Go to the theater. Rent a movie. Check out that new comedienne at the comedy club. Share the laughter by asking another couple to join you and your partner.
- Learn to relax and let go more. Life's not that serious.
- Think back on a time when somebody told you something that made you just start whoopin'. Now, that was funny!
- Share a funny story with someone today—your children, your wife, your pops, your sister. Spread the good humor.

77. Invite the kid in you to come out to play.

It's an emergency for me to learn how to play. It is something I don't know how to do. I've never just taken time off and played.

—Bernice Johnson Reagon, musician, curator, historian, author, and civil-rights activist

Seems as though we don't appreciate the many joys of childhood until we reach adulthood. Welcome to a world where responsibilities are never-ending. Yet as children we couldn't wait to do what grown-ups do. Couldn't wait to stay out all night. Couldn't wait to drive a car. Couldn't wait to vote.

Couldn't wait to buy our first drink. Little did we know. Then, what seemed like a life filled with freedom and adventure, soon came to pass. And reality eventually set in.

Sometimes we believe that being a "grown-up" means putting ourselves last, or we believe we are too busy to play. What would happen if we lavished attention on ourselves? What kind of men would that make us?

Actually, we adults can learn a lot from children. They know how to play hard. Contrary to what we might believe, even as adults, we can loosen our collars and ties and play just as hard if we let the kid in us come out sometimes.

Revisiting our childhood might mean taking your children to the park and letting them push *you* on the swing for a change. It might mean pulling out your old skates for a skate date with your honey. How about planning a trip to the amusement park to ride your favorite roller coaster again? Or inviting the old gang over tonight for a game of Twister or a competitive game of UNO, marbles, or charades. Whether you play adult games or games from your youth, just have big fun. Play hard! Really hard!

Action Steps

- Have your children, little nephews, or nieces teach you how to play Nintendo games. After all, you used to *reign* as the Space Invaders and Atari king back in the day!

- Catch one of your favorite cartoons on the Cartoon Channel or tune in to "Nick at Nite" for blast-from-the-past episodes of your favorite sitcoms.

- Buy that bicycle you've been eying for some time now. Then check out the new cycling paths in your area. Take the family and make a day of it.

- Pick up a box of the favorite cereal you ate as a kid. It'll probably taste better than ever, since you haven't had it in years.

- Next time they're out, catch a few lightning bugs in a jar. They're still around, and they still display that bright yellow glow that used to fascinate you. (But don't forget to set them free again!)

78. Seek to be understood by the sister.

Men may be from Mars and we womenfolks from Venus. But we have got to figure out how to live better with each other right here on earth.

—Johnnetta B. Cole, former president of Spelman College

Brothers, it's time to stop playing the mystery game of "Who Am I?" If we are to enjoy happy, healthy relationships with our mates, we've got to get comfortable and secure enough to begin sharing the real us with them. That means communicating honestly and effectively our hopes, our desires, our needs, and our fears. Only then can we expect reciprocity in the relationship.

Peeling back protective layers to reveal what makes us tick doesn't rob us of our inner selves. It allows us to share with those we love a wonderful side of ourselves we seldom reveal. Traditionally we have not let others in very easily. It's still hard today for some men. The personal struggles we brothers experience sometimes cause us to keep our hearts under tight surveillance. We're very cautious about who we trust and in whom we confide.

In our quest to make our sisters understand us as brothers, let us invite them into our minds and hearts for sincere love, truth, and mutual understanding. As a people, we have conquered much in the face of a society that has sought to destroy us.

How-to books do have their place. Relationship magazines

can surely enlighten. However, in our efforts to understand one another as unique individuals, we have to look beyond the written word and have heart-to-heart, candid dialogue with those with whom we are intimate and share love. Establishing lines of communication with the special ladies in our lives is a good start to unfolding many a mystery.

Action Steps

- Share with your mate an issue with which you've been struggling. Explain how it's been making you feel. Ask her to help you work through it. Decide on a team approach to lifting your burden.

- Share your greatest fear with your mate, and explore ways you may seek to overcome it.

- Having problems with your mate? Talk to your mother about her relationship with your father. Ask her for some how-to advice on how to cope and conquer. More than likely, she's been there and done that, and is willing to extend a helping hand to her "baby."

79. Seek to understand the sister.

> Along the way, I rediscovered my wife's strengths, her vulnerabilities, and her most cherished hopes and dreams. I released the ego-inflating notion that she needed me in her life, and I chose, rather, to celebrate that she wanted me there.
>
> —Dr. Ronn Elmore, author, psychotherapist, and minister

We've been told we are from Mars and they are from Venus. Whether that's true or not, it sure seems that way at times. As the battle between the sexes rages on, black men still have a hard time understanding the sisters. And they *can* be tough to figure out. What gives them an edge over us, though, is that they put forth a much greater effort to try to understand us.

Women, in general, have been reading about men for quite some time now. They're learning our likes and dislikes, what makes us tick, and why we do the things we do. Not only are they reading, but they're writing manuals on how to marry us, rule books on how to keep us at bay, and articles on how to make us better lovers.

Thing is, you'd think by now we'd have a clue and start seeking to better understand them. Come on, troops. The women are way ahead of us in the game. Only when we begin to express an interest in learning more about what they want, what they like, and what makes them tick can we Martians and Venutians come together with a newfound understanding. Just think how well we'd complement each other when we're equipped with the knowledge of how to fulfill each others' wants and desires the way we should.

Action Steps

- Subscribe to women's magazines such as *O, The Oprah Magazine; Essence;* and *Today's Black Woman.* Many women's magazines have a for-brothers-only column that speaks to men.

- If you're in the dark about it, ask a woman you're close to explain to you all about PMS, periods, and yeast infections. If you're an older brother who back in the day didn't talk about things like this, get over it; times have changed, and you need to know about these facts of life. The days of ignorance for fear of embarrassment are over. You very well might need to explain these things to your son or daughter one day. So, you better know the facts.

- Subscribe to and read men's magazines, such as *Maxim* and *Just for Black Men,* which contain articles on relationships with the women in our lives.

- Read some of the many books women are reading about their experiences as black women. Titles you might pick up include *Waiting to Exhale*, by Terry McMillan; *Just Between Girlfriends*, by Chrisena Coleman, *The Women of Brewster Place*, by Gloria Naylor; and *Souls of My Sisters: Black Women Break Their Silence, Tell Their Stories, and Heal Their Spirit*, by Dawn Marie Daniels and Candace Sandy. No, you won't agree with everything in these pages, but the books will provide you with other perspectives.

80. Be trustworthy and dependable.

Think carefully before you promise to do something. Once you say you'll do it, you'll have to do it.
—The Delany Sisters, authors

There is much to be praised about a person you can trust, a person you can depend on. When there is trust, the depth of a relationship becomes greater. Friends become tighter. Mates feel closer. Colleagues connect. Teachers believe. Whether in business, social, or academic life, being pegged as "trustworthy" and "dependable" are great labels to have placed upon you. In essence, being trustworthy and dependable boils down to you keeping your word. Here's what one dictionary entry for *trustworthy* reads:

trust·wor·thy *adjective*. Warranting trust; reliable. See synonyms at RELIABLE.

Now, here's what it reads for *dependable*:

de·pend·a·ble *adjective*. Trustworthy. See synonyms at RELIABLE.

So, as you can read from the definitions, the characterizations go hand in hand. In a world that seems to be filled with back-stabbing, it's a pleasure and joy to know someone you can trust. Really trust. Old sayings like "One good turn deserves another" couldn't be more true. If you are to find a trustworthy and dependable person, he or she is going to have to find you in the same light.

Remember, if you were to lose it all today—the money, the good life, your health—your word remains golden. When a man loses that, he has little else.

A word on dependability: Being there when it counts is what it's all about. It can be something as simple as getting to work on time or making sure you're at the bedside of a friend or family member before and after surgery.

Being trustworthy and dependable is like a good golf swing—ya gotta follow through, man. Ya gotta follow through!

Action Steps

- Develop trust and honesty in relationships. These are the keys to a successful one.
- Always keep your word.
- Don't make a promise you know you can't keep.
- Don't be a "dependable deadbeat." For example, if you find that you're unable to come through, tell a person up front. A good way to damage your trustworthiness and dependability is allowing a person to think you're taking care of business, but then not to follow through.

81. Be a pioneer.

[Black golfers] Charlie Sifford, Lee Elder, Ted Rhodes—
those are the guys who paved the way for me . . .
Coming up on the eighteen [hole], I said a little prayer of
thanks to those guys. Those guys are the ones who did it.
—Tiger Woods, athlete

Someone has to be first. Why not you?

Being a pioneer is nothing new in the African-American community. To get a glimpse you only need to drive your car down the street and stop at a traffic light, invented by brother Garrett A. Morgan. Go to a hospital to see the blood-bank legacy of Dr. Charles Drew. Pick up a jar of peanut butter to see George Washington Carver's genius.

What we need today are more pioneers. More Morgans, more Drews, more Carvers.

Each man who is born has an untouched talent to discover something new. It can be a new way of writing; it can be a new sports technique on the golf course or baseball diamond; or it can be organizing a group to travel to a future Million Man March. Whatever it is, we black men must become pioneers once more.

For every James Brown, there must be a new pioneer establishing exciting ways to entertain the masses.

For every Rev. Dr. Martin Luther King Jr., there must be a new pioneer leading our people.

For every General Colin Powell, there must be a new pioneer to pick up the torch where the general left off in defending this great country we call home.

For every Reginald Lewis, there must be a new pioneer who can break the glass ceilings of corporate America.

For every Willie Brown, there must be a new pioneer who can stand tall and strong in the midst of political winds.

A pioneer is a leader, a beginner, someone who sets the

tone, the pace, and paves the road. We African-American men have many new roads to travel. They won't be paved, however, unless we have new pioneers. These new pioneers must be ready and willing to tear up the sod and make a road with the strength of concrete, the flexibility of asphalt, and the durability of a speedway.

Action Steps

- Develop skills that can help you start something new.
- Seek more creativity in your work.
- Don't be second when you could be first.
- Talk with the living pioneers of our day. You can't teach an old dog new tricks, but the old dogs can teach you a few.

82. Stand up and be counted.

This is your future—don't leave it blank.
—Census 2000 slogan

Every ten years in America each of us has a chance to be counted, but so many of us miss out. We all have a chance to be counted during the census.

Stand up, black man! Be counted! Your ancestors fought hard to ensure that you have a presence on this planet. Make it known!

While some of us have been suspicious about answering the questions on the U.S. census forms, it is imperative that we participate. The federal government uses the count to distribute millions of dollars to our communities and also to decide how many congressional representatives our communities will have.

If there ever was a time to stand for something, it is the

year of the census. Black communities have complained about being undercounted during the past few censuses. The only way to avoid this problem is to participate. Everyone should be counted. Remember, there is strength in numbers.

Action Steps

- Participate in every census.

- Explain to friends and relatives the importance of being counted in censuses.

- Vote in the next local, state, and national election. Show yourself.

- Read books on the contributions of African Americans to the building of the United States of America.

83. Be an expert on something.

The more I know, the more I know I don't know.
—Unknown

How many times have you watched a television news show when the anchor is interviewing an expert? How many times was a black man that expert? Probably not many. There is really no excuse for this, for there are many black experts out there, yet we need them to be more visible.

You, too, can become an expert or authority on something. All it takes is for you to decide what interests you and seek to learn all you can about the subject. Be it in the area of politics, energy, economic policy, robotics, nuclear weapons, relationships, or space, start reading and talking to folks who are in the know.

When you are an authority on a topic, you can command respect in our society, and you will have an edge when you are applying for jobs in professional arenas. When it comes time for *Nightline* to call on an expert, the pool of talented blacks should be full, and it will be once more of us begin working to become the next expert produced by the black community.

Action Steps

- Take up a hobby and become fully knowledgeable about it.
- Learn a new trade and know everything there is to know about it.
- Work with other brothers on ways to help each of you become an authority.

84. Understand the meaning of the word *no.*

What part of the word no *don't you understand—the* n *or the* o?

—Unknown

In today's achieve-at-all-costs society, we are often told to not let anything stop us from getting what we want. Motivational speakers, self-help gurus, and magazine articles tell us we can have it all, anytime we want it. "When others tell you 'no,' you say next!" they tell us. Sure, we can achieve anything we want if we put our minds to it. But we must keep the word *no* in the proper perspective, in the right context. This is especially important to do when it comes to potentially violating the rights of other people.

Brothers, if a woman with whom you're being intimate says "no" to moving to "the next base," take your hand out of there, get off of her, and honor her request! Rape is an ugly, inhuman, and serious crime. If your parent says "no," to your request, don't challenge, don't beg, don't back-talk—

go somewhere and sit down! And if the sign says "NO TRES-PASSING," stay out! If the police officer tells you not to move, obey. Simple as that.

Much too frequently, our don't-take-no-for-an-answer attitude lands us in court, out of favor, and in jail. We can save ourselves a lot of man-made headaches if we just respect the word *no*.

Action Steps

- Don't try to strong-arm others to get your own way.

- Know that "no" means "no." It doesn't mean the person wants you to keep doing it, to keep going—it simply means "no"!

- Keep the meaning of *no* in the right perspective.

- Know how to tell others "no." Remember, you always have the right to say "no" if you feel something compromises your integrity, morals, values, or principles.

- Read the book *Understanding the Tin Man: Why So Many Men Avoid Intimacy*, by William July II.

85. Remember where you came from.

The fruit must have a stem before it grows.

—Jabo (Liberia) proverb

Many brothers believe that once you make it, you need not look back. This is a mistake. It is always helpful to know where you came from. By not losing sight of where you've been, you'll be better able to direct where you're going.

The saying "Those who forget history are condemned to repeat it" fits perfectly here in that if we don't remember where we came from, we may just end up back there.

While climbing the ladder of success, make sure you look back to see if you can lend a helping hand to another brother or sister. If he or she chooses to climb with you, right on! If not, you keep moving onward and upward—knowing that you did offer to help.

Also, don't forget, brothers, the folks back home are always looking for hometown heroes, brothers of whom they can be proud. Don't dis them by forgetting them. When you get a chance, stop home and talk with the folks who helped pave the way for you, and don't forget to say thank you.

Action Steps

- Write letters to the folks in your hometown.
- Volunteer to be a part of a hometown alumni group.
- Go back home and give motivational speeches and talk with young people.
- Donate money or time to help out in your community.

86. Be flexible.

A tree stays rooted, but a tree knows how to bend.
—Tina Turner, entertainer

Flexibility is an attribute many of us brothers have but often don't put to good use. By being flexible, you allow yourself room to maneuver, room to grow, room to shape yourself into a better person.

Imagine that the Lakers had only Shaquille O'Neal, four other players, and no bench. The coach would only win about three-fourths of the games the team wins each year. However, with a bench, the coach can be flexible. The coach can give Shaq some rest time. He can move around players to match up the team's offense against the opponent's defense. You get the picture. Even with Shaq, the team needs flexibility to succeed as greatly as it has.

We can easily adapt this example to our everyday lives. If we allow ourselves to be flexible, we open the floodgates of possibilities, opportunities, and choices we never thought we had.

In dealing with others, it pays to be flexible. At work, for example, be flexible at times when the boss needs you to come in early. The boss might remember you were flexible when bonus time comes around. And make sure the boss doesn't forget that you were flexible when you need him or her to be flexible.

Action Steps

- Know that flexibility is an attribute, not a fault.
- Do a chore today that normally your wife does, giving her the time to do something she enjoys.
- Be willing to make adjustments in your life. A few changes here and there doesn't mean the end of the world.

87. Leave a legacy.

*I used to want the words "She Tried" on my tombstone.
Now I want "She Did It."*

— Katherine Dunham, choreographer and dancer

If you died tonight, what would they say at your funeral? How would your eulogy read? What would you want on your tombstone? Your own mortality isn't something you probably give much thought to, but consider this: Would your eulogy reflect you as a loving and compassionate man who was dedicated to his family? Or a mean-spirited son of a bitch who cared only for himself? A giving man on whom you can depend? Or an irresponsible, unpredictable guy who failed to do what he said he'd do? A spiritual man who respected his higher power? Or a devilish soul without reverence for the Creator?

How about your tombstone—would it simply read REST IN PEACE?

How others remember us after we're gone depends largely on the lives we live today. How are you living today?

Action Steps

- Grab a pen and a piece of paper. Now, write down the title of your autobiography.
- Write an honest obituary for yourself.
- Give some thought today about what you could do to better your life.

88. Don't smoke.

> SURGEON GENERAL'S WARNING: Smoking Causes Lung Cancer, Heart Disease, Emphysema and May Complicate Pregnancy.
>
> —U.S. Surgeon General's Office

This concept is an easy one, a no-brainer. It's been proven that smoking can aid in killing you, so why cut your life short?

A man's wife was in her early forties when she was diagnosed with cancer. She was an educator, smart, intelligent, beautiful, and radiant. Yet her twenty-plus years of smoking had a debilitating effect on her. Within two years of being diagnosed with cancer, she was gone—that fast! She put all of her academic skills to use, spending every waking moment learning about cancer and ways to fight it. She fought a good fight and lasted two years longer than any of the doctors had expected. However, if she had not been a smoker, she might still be with us today. Her family and friends suffered a great loss of a very special person. So, the unhealthy choice made by an intelligent woman left loved ones with the consequence of deep sorrow.

It may be easy for someone who never started smoking to tell others to just stop. Doing so, however, really isn't that easy—even in the midst of hundreds of thousands of examples like the one above. The nicotine in cigarettes is addictive—plain and simple. The tobacco companies, after much legal haggling, have even confessed to this truth. Trying to "break the habit" can be a serious struggle. Many smokers are concerned that they might gain weight after they quit. It's a possibility. Being a bit heavier is, though, a far "better" problem to deal with than lung cancer.

It's not easy to stop smoking, something nonsmokers don't always understand. Nevertheless, nonsmokers should continually encourage friends and loved ones who smoke to try to kick the habit. They may not care to hear about the ills of smoking, but if nonsmokers don't remind them—albeit gently, or at times harshly—who will? The tobacco companies?

Action Steps

- Think twice before you light up.
- Remember, secondhand smoke affects not only the smoker, but all others around the smoker.
- Never, ever ask a child to go buy you a pack of cigarettes. Not only is it illegal, the last thing you want to do is provide a child with any reason to try smoking.
- Know that if you smoke, you are one of many men who face an earlier death.

- Know that cigarette smoking *isn't* cool. Smoking may have looked cool, especially if you bought into all the movie, television, and print campaigns, but it really never was. Fellas, smoking will kill you now just as it always has. Warnings not to smoke are nothing new. We are just now more aware of the dangers.

89. Never use illegal drugs.

Don't fool with drugs or folks who do drugs. They have nothing to offer you but trouble.

—The Delany Sisters, authors

If you didn't see the movie *Jungle Fever*, truck to the video store to rent it. It is a film about the underworld operations of very savvy drug lords and how drugs take over a neighborhood. A key part of the movie is when the character played by Samuel L. Jackson (before he became a major star) is so addicted to drugs that he steals his aging mother's television set to pawn for money to buy more dope. This scene stands out as the very essence of what drugs can lead you to do: to steal from your own family.

If you think smoking cigarettes is addictive, smoking illegal drugs is much, much worse. Most crime these days is tied to drugs. Drug users who run out of money—who can't steal their own mother's TV set—will steal yours, and everything else they can, to get their next fix.

Aside from the effects drug use and drug abuse has on our communities, drug use and abuse has ultradamaging effects on the human body. Crack cocaine, LSD, heroin, and marijuana all have been proven to do ill to the body.

If you care about being somebody, being a success, not being on the bottom rung of society, then you should "just say no." Mean it. The old adage, "Don't knock it till you try it" doesn't work here—at all. First and foremost, using drugs is against the law, and it goes against any common sense if you are concerned about your and your loved ones' health, safety, and happiness.

Action Steps

- Know that knowledge is power, and you eliminate your power when you fry your brain on drugs. Using drugs reduces your brain's capacity to absorb information.

- Stop falling prey to the images on TV and in movies that glamorize the drug world.

- Remember, no drug dealer, pusher, or drug ringleader has ever retired from the industry.

- Don't start! A first-time crack user can get hooked immediately.

- Beware! Heroin is once again rearing its ugly head in the drug world.

- Although there is a great debate over the dangers versus the curing power of marijuana, keep away from it. Let medical professionals decide when it should be legally used.

- If they're doing drugs where you are, leave. Simply say, "See ya." Being pegged as an accomplice is a man-made headache you can do without.

90. Be willing to share the spotlight.

*The record [at Grambling State University] belongs to
everybody, all the former players, all the assistant
coaches and all the loyal fans that have supported
Grambling throughout the years. Eddie Robinson sure
hasn't done it alone.*

—Eddie Robinson, former football coach
of Grambling State University

Accomplishment. Success. Admiration. Fame. Victory. These
are things that can make us feel good inside. To show others
we did it, that we made it happen, gives us a sense of pride
and self-achievement. Having our fifteen minutes of fame
can be fun, exciting, and do wonders for the self-esteem. Notice the key words *our* and *we*. Yet to hog the spotlight without giving others their due is to put on a false front. Sometimes in our roles as team captains, chairmen, supervisors,
and presidents, we fail to recognize the work of the foot
soldiers who helped get us where we are.

Acknowledging those who were instrumental to our success doesn't mean compromising our pride or sense of
achievement. Rather, it tells them we appreciate them and
their support. Next time you're in charge of pulling off the
big event, or accepting the honor, take inventory of those
around you who helped to make it all possible. Then step
aside to let them bask in the spotlight too. Without them,
standing center stage can be a lonely place.

Action Steps

- Make a conscious effort to give credit where credit is due.

- Know that it's okay to share your successes with others; just
be careful not to brag.

- Invite family members, friends, and associates to help you with a project. Remember, sometimes multiple heads are better than one.

- Reward your volunteers with tokens of affection or appreciation, keeping in mind they don't have to be lavish gifts.

- Send thank-you notes to express gratitude.

- Be as happy for others' successes as you are for your own.

91. Network.

A single bracelet does not jingle.

—African (Congo) proverb

A *net* is defined as something made of openwork fabric, especially a device for capturing birds, fish, or insects, or something that entraps; a snare.

Work is defined as physical or mental effort or activity directed toward the production or accomplishment of something; or something that one is doing, making, or performing, especially as an occupation or undertaking; a duty or task.

So, when you put *net* and *work* together, you get a person who is busy putting his physical or mental ability in gear to produce a net designed to snare or grab something. For our purposes here, what we're grabbing are contacts. Contacts can mean so much to you in your quest for a better life— principally through a better career.

Black people often take for granted how many contacts we have and often don't use the ones we've developed. Each year at various conventions and conferences of black professional organizations, participants bring their business cards. They pass them out. They write their home phone numbers on the back for added convenience to keep in touch. They tell their new contact, "I'll give you a call!" Then, when next year rolls around, they realize they haven't called a soul. So much for building that network.

The rule is simple. When you meet someone new who can help you out (and vice versa), don't wait to get in touch, do it immediately—while you still remember the person clearly. Also, it's a good idea to snap a photo with the person to help recall who handed you that fancy business card.

Remember, there is much truth to the saying, "It's not what you know, but who you know;" but if you don't work your network, you'll be a brother with a whole lot of "what" and very little "who"—which won't get you any "where" these days.

Action Steps

- Join professional organizations, and develop your network within the groups.

- Keep in close contact with business colleagues. It's a waste of time to write information on the back of a business card that you'll never use.

- Be active in events and activities around the city, state, and country. Never limit your networking ability by reaching out only locally.

- Network with colleagues, fraternal friends, and civic friends around the globe. Remember, the world is getting smaller every day.

92. Take the time to meditate.

I've got a lot of work to do with my life but I feel good that at this age what I'm most concerned about is finding inner peace.

—Sean "P. Diddy" Combs, entertainer

Me? Meditate? Yeah, right! you may be thinking. Wait. Read on. Here's some news you can use, brother.

With all its ups and downs, life can be rough sometimes. On some days, in fact, it's all we can do to not throw our hands up in the air in discouragement, disgust, and dismay. "What else can go wrong?" we ask. Without an answer in return, we usually go on about our daily round, never knowing how to deal with the crises that plague us.

What if there were a "magic" method to help you deal with the madness—would you jump at the chance? If you answered yes, then listen up. Though not magic, meditation is one of the oldest known religious practices. Some form of it has been practiced in virtually every religion in the world since time began. As African Americans, many of us, especially men, may not be aware of the many benefits of the practice, or we may view it as something out of sync with the natural rhythm of black folk. Nothing is further from the truth. In fact, contrary to popular belief, meditation doesn't require you to do yoga, be a monk, or even be a "God-fearing religious man"— Buddhist, Christian, or otherwise—to reap its astounding benefits. Today, meditation is used by many brothers and sisters who aren't religious as a method of stress reduction.

Meditation is a state of deep physical relaxation coupled with a mental state in which the mind is focused on a single point of reference. It can also be a means of invoking divine grace. Informal meditation can be anything that quiets your mind: Stretching just before your workout at the gym. Fishing. Jogging. Gardening. Swimming. Woodworking. Painting. Writing. Polishing a car. Walking in the woods or on the beach. Cooking. Making or listening to music. Formal meditation requires concentrated discipline. It has lots of physical, mental, and spiritual benefits, but most importantly it can produce profound and blissful relaxation. Meditating daily can do wonders for your mind, body, and soul.

Meditation is a practice that can enable us to understand

everything in our lives more clearly. Individually, it allows us to examine what is happening to ourselves, and it can help us to get to know ourselves in order to transform and reveal our lives in a new perspective. As African-American men, we can certainly benefit from the rewards of meditation. Given the stress we face each and every day, we should do all we can to quiet our minds, lower our blood pressure, and develop a greater sense of inner peace.

You can even incorporate a personal mantra into your daily meditation routine. What's a mantra? It's a word, sound, prayer, phrase, or muscular activity that you repeat to yourself over and over again to induce a meditative state. The process has been practiced for years around the world, but not until fairly recent times did it become accepted by the Western scientific community as a valid medical tool. Today, mantra meditation is used to treat patients in hospitals and clinics across the country to reduce stress, lower blood pressure, and reduce the risk of heart disease and stroke—illnesses common to black men. This is the scientific reason why reciting "left-right-left-right" helps soldiers march farther, that drum-beating is a central part of African healing, that relaxing in Grandmama's rocking chair is so soothing. Mantra meditation can be compared to a Swiss army knife; it, too, can do many things by allowing all the propensities of a person to come to the surface and expand. We can accomplish this by gaining increased control over our mind, senses, emotions, and ultimately our lives.

Before you move on, give this a quick try: Close your eyes; then take five deep breaths; each time you exhale, imagine you are breathing away worries and anxieties. With a little daily repetition, you'll be on your way to the serene lifestyle you deserve.

Action Steps

- Open your mind to new practices.
- Pick up a book or audio book on meditation at the library or bookstore.
- Find out if a meditation class is offered in your area. If so, enroll.
- Talk to other men who meditate; they'll tell you how it's worked for them.
- Try doing deep-breathing exercises.
- This week, don't talk on the phone, deal with coworkers, or run errands during your lunch break. Meditate instead.
- Practice meditating away from others in the house; find a quiet spot.
- Learn to meditate, then teach your children and wife.

93. Know that everything is not about competition.

A man with too much ambition cannot sleep in peace.

—African proverb (Baguirmi)

In America we have been conditioned to believe that everything is about competing and winning. It is the basis of a capitalistic society. Competition is at the core of our very being in this country. In the corporate world, we talk about who won and who lost on Wall Street at the close of the stock exchanges each day. In sports, we keep a daily tab of a team's wins and losses. At college, it's not important that the players graduate, it's whether or not they're contenders for a national championship. In television, it's always a ratings game—who's watching whom depends on who wins. That may be the way it is—but that's not the way it ought to be.

If we, especially as black brothers, continue to feed the frenzy that everything is based on winning or losing, we will eventually all lose. We will lose the idea of comradeship, brotherhood, and the joy of "playing the game."

Remember, it's okay to compete; that's good for the soul. Like anything else in life, though, too much of anything is usually bad for you. Competition is no different.

Action Steps

- Compete but with a level head; put competition into perspective.

- Develop new ways of competing with your fellow man. He and you both stand to grow and develop if you try new ways to compete.

- This week work on a strategy that allows you to compete with honor.

- Know that losing is not the end of the world. It just means you are able to compete another day.

- Go a week without teasing.

94. Learn a foreign language.

Mastery of language affords remarkable power.
—Frantz Fanon, psychiatrist, philosopher, and political activist

"He who knows no other tongue, knows nothing of his own." This saying can't be more true. Many Americans, both white and black, think knowing English is enough. It isn't. At one time that may have been sufficient to succeed. As the world gets smaller every day, it becomes paramount that African Americans learn the languages of other peoples.

Take Spanish, for example. If the U.S. Census Bureau's figures hold up, the majority of the minorities in this country will soon be Hispanics. In a few years, more than 35 percent of all Americans will speak it as their first language. Also, if you plan to do any business in Central or South America, you can do a whole lot more if you know the language of the people there. Plus, you won't have to pay for an interpreter. Save the bucks and speak their language.

Learning French is important too. Should you travel to Europe, you'll find it easier to get around if you know this language.

Been in an airport lately? If you stop at the international information desk, you'll run into folks who know four or five languages.

The key here is to know that even though English is viewed by the rest of the world as the premier language to know, it can only help you personally and professionally to speak other languages.

It is very important to have the knowledge and skills to communicate effectively in other languages, to connect to other disciplines, and to compare our cultures to others in order to better understand the communities of the world.

Action Steps

- A year from now, know a foreign language.

- Go for Baroque! Increase your value in corporate America by mastering Spanish, French, *and* Japanese! Be multilingual. Most companies today conduct business with international clients and/or have offices overseas. Guess who could be chosen to meet with executives from other countries, or even selected to attend overseas business meetings!

- Try out your new language on your wife or girlfriend. It's been said some women love a man who's multilingual—especially in the Romance-language department (Spanish, French, and Italian).

- Take an evening course through a community college's continuing education program. These classes often include people who have not taken a class before, or who took foreign-language courses years ago and want to refresh. You'll be in good company, with plenty of people to study with outside of class.

- Listen to radio stations and watch cable or satellite networks that air foreign-language programming. It's a great way to pick up on a new language. Listen to comprehend.

95. Maintain high self-esteem.

If you have no confidence in self, you are twice defeated in the race of life. With confidence, you have won even before you have started.

—Marcus Garvey, black-nationalist leader

In this often busy world we live in, it's rare that someone will go out of his way to give you a pat on the back. However, that shouldn't stop you from keeping your spirits high. Hard work and hard play usually pay off, even if we can't see the payoff coming.

The Rev. Charles G. Adams of Detroit's Hartford Memorial Baptist Church was delivering the commencement address at Dillard University one scorching summer day in New Orleans. He put the idea of self-esteem best in part of his address to the graduates:

"When you get knocked down, get back up!"
"When you get put in a corner, and you're on the ropes, come out swinging."

"Never give up. Never give up!"
"When a mountain's in your way, climb it!"

What Reverend Adams was preaching about is self-reliance and the ability to keep on keepin' on—even in the darkest hour, in the worst of times. The ability to do this adds to your character, adds to your self-esteem.

Self-esteem is so important because if we don't say to ourselves once in a while, "job well done," no one else will. However, to do this, each man of color in today's society must be willing to be the very best he can be at whatever he "bes."

The Rev. Dr. Martin Luther King Jr. said it best when he noted: "If it falls your lot to be a street sweeper, sweep streets as Raphael painted pictures, sweep streets as Michelangelo carved marble, sweep streets as Beethoven composed music, or Shakespeare wrote poetry."

Action Steps

- Always hold your head up high—no matter what.
- Don't listen when others tell you you're nothing. They're wrong.
- Turn away when others try to tear you down. It is they who will be torn down. No one succeeds in his or her own construction while busily working to deconstruct others' goals and ambitions.
- Know you are special, brother!

96. Confront your fears.

Fear is not a wall, but an emotion. And like all emotions, it can be overcome.

—Dr. Gwendolyn Goldsby Grant, psychologist and author

"What are you afraid of? It's not gonna hurt you." As boys we heard this a thousand times from the other kids in the neighborhood, in gym class, or on the playground at school. Sometimes even adults told us this to allow the doctor to give us the shot, let Mom pull out the splinter, or get us to finally dive into the pool. Some fears we outgrow. Others we don't. Guess what? They continue to be legitimate for many men. That's okay. They're real fears, and they're ours.

Today, as adult men—some with children of our own— there are still things that frighten us. Riding on an airplane. Snakes. Committed relationships. Success. Connecting with your spirit. Computers. Spiders. Becoming our authentic selves. Admitting mistakes. Riding a roller coaster.

Traditionally men have not been given permission to acknowledge what makes us uncomfortable, afraid, or even frightens us to death. We are taught at an early age to be fearless, strong, and to comfort the fears of others. This is why grown men rarely disclose our fears to our mates, our children, our parents, our coworkers. We hide what unnerves us or makes us downright squeamish. We resort to hiding our fears behind our best suit of armor to impress those for whom we think we have to be strong.

No matter how well hidden they are, fears remain in our hearts and our minds. As mature men, we must deal openly and honestly with them. This week, give some thought to the deepest anxieties you have quietly tucked away for fear of being condemned or thought of as "unmanly" by others. Write them down; then plan your strategy for tackling them head-on to begin to erase them from your life.

Do keep in mind, however, that there is a difference between the things we fear and things that flat-out don't appeal to us. Recognize the difference between the two.

Action Steps

- Let your children—girls and boys—know that it's okay for them to feel scared, squeamish, or terrified of something. When they experience something frightening, talk about it openly with them. Share your fears with them, so that they know that adults get scared sometimes, too.
- Do something today that you've been dreading for some time now. Go on. Get it over with. The sooner you get out what's stuck in your craw, the better you'll feel. You'll begin to feel the burden lifting immediately.
- Share your innermost fears with your mate, best friend, or confidant. He or she might be able to help you work through them.
- Come to grips with the fact that even *you* have fears or things that make you uncomfortable—and it doesn't mean you're weak. It means you're human.

97. If it's "hot," don't touch it!

He who profits by a crime commits it.

—Unknown

Possession of stolen goods is against the law, plain and simple. That alone should be enough to deter anyone from buying something that someone else got as a "five-finger discount."

We should not consider only those items as "hot," but also all of those bootleg items one can pick up on many big-city street corners. When we buy bootleg copies of music—audiocassettes and CDs from bootleggers—again, we are breaking the law. You also hurt the efforts of artists who earn a living based on how many recordings they sell. The quality of bootleg goods usually is not as good as the original. You deserve better. If something doesn't look or sound as good as it should, you usually can't get your money back.

Stealing never feels right. Our consciences tell us that. Can you live with it? That is the question. If your answer is a resounding *yes*, you need to rethink the way you are living. Making honest purchases from honest vendors is not only the right thing to do, it's the legal thing to do. There are enough of us in jail already.

So, remember, if it's "hot," don't touch it. You will get burned!

Action Steps

- Never take part in the economic enterprises of criminals—no matter how sweet the deal may seem.
- Support hard-working businesspeople who sell legitimate goods.
- Instill in your small children and their playmates the need to work hard to earn the things they want in life.

98. Be one of the "good men."

Reputation is made in a moment. Character is built in a lifetime.

—Unknown

The media in America today often focus on women who can't seem to find "a good man," as though they were the only ones looking for meaningful relationships. What's interesting, however, is that there are a lot of men out there looking for exactly the same thing. Single men. Divorced men. Widowed men. Lonely men. They're out there—yep, even black men. They're not all jobless, in jail, or on drugs. Many are looking for the love of a good woman. Truth be told, men's journey to find the right mate can be just as difficult as women's. Yet talk shows, magazine articles, and statistical data would have you believe differently.

Some men, like women, become so frustrated in the quest, they retreat. That doesn't have to be our fate, brothers. There are a lot of "good men" among us who are just waiting to be loved, caressed, and cuddled after a long day at work. Men eager to be fathers to children of their own. Men more than willing to be full-time, stay-at-home daddies to their babies. Men aching to pray with, lean on, and wake up with the same woman day after day. These brothers are looking for mates who want the same.

Have you ever just wanted to shout aloud, "Open your eyes, woman. I'm here! Are ya blind?"

Action Steps

- Not meeting your woman of choice in places you've been looking? Try other venues, such as your house of worship, community gatherings, the health club, or wedding receptions. These places are full of "good women."

- Steer clear of the escort and dating services and 900 numbers. It's highly unlikely you'll find the woman of your dreams taking that route.

- Talk with single female friends or relatives who are looking for their ideal man. Ask them what qualities they're seeking. You're sure to get an earful—and probably learn a few things too!

- Check out http://www.agoodblackman.com. It's an *awesome* on-line magazine dedicated to uplifting, empowering, and celebrating men of African descent by providing brothers (and the women who love them) with a place for information and inspiration.

99. Have the patience of Job.

I know the Lord will help. But help me, Lord, until you help.

—Hasidic prayer

In the Bible, the book of Job tells the story of a righteous man who loses everything. The story presents an unusual beginning, in which Satan talks God into trying to break Job to see if Job will turn against God. As a result, Job's faith is tested over and over again. In a string of catastrophes, raiders steal some of his vast herds, and an unexplained fire descending from heaven torches and demolishes the rest; a violent windstorm destroys his home, killing his ten children inside; then Job's body is mysteriously covered from head to toe with unsightly sores.

Friends visit Job in the midst of all his woes to comfort and advise him. Although sympathetic, they argue that surely a tragedy of such magnitude is some type of punishment for Job for some sin he's committed. They strongly urged him to confess what he's done, but Job stands firm, maintaining his innocence—that he has not sinned—but he is dismayed that God could be so unjust. He even wonders aloud why he can't plead directly with God.

Finally, God answers Job's call from a whirlwind, but not for the purpose of explaining the tragic events that have occurred. Rather, over the course of two chapters in the story, God speaks to Job about the wonders of Creation. Job responds by acknowledging that he was wrong to challenge God's actions or inactions.

The story concludes with God blessing Job with ten more children and great wealth and prosperity beyond Job's wildest dreams.

The first question most of us ask is why God allowed Job to be the "guinea pig" in a wager between God and Satan.

Obviously, Job was just minding his business being an up-right man. The first time Satan attempts to break Job, it doesn't work. He still follows God but eventually starts questioning Him.

Have you ever felt like a modern-day Job? When some unforeseen event, some "simple twist of fate" brought you face-to-face with you own private horror? How did you handle it? Did you break? Or did you see the other side? It's when you hit rock-bottom that your strength is tested, just like Job's was. Still, Job hung tough, despite everything he endured—theft, destruction, tragic losses of loved ones, and ill health. He remained patient and steadfast—but not without frustration. Although an honorable man, his human nature kicked in and he questioned God.

Bad things happen even to good men. We don't always understand the whys and the hows of what we're put through in life. Maybe it's not for us to question or to ever understand. One thing we do know is that, like Job, men who have suffered their greatest losses, their worst tragedies, have later been blessed with richer lives and great prosperity.

Bible scholars call God's speeches the Divine Speeches. These speeches serve to meet the innocent sufferer at the level of the fear of abandonment and forgetfulness, and to give reassurance of divine remembrance and presence. Scholars have even suggested that the story of Job is probably a metaphor for the nation of Israel, questioning why God made its people suffer so hard for so long. In the book of Job, the idea of reward and punishment is seen, and a righteous man suffers for no reason. Unfortunately, the story of Job doesn't really answer the question of why, but it helps us to know that a higher power is somehow capable of understanding even when we don't.

When bad things happen to you, you may be dismayed, you may cry, you may feel beaten, you may not understand.

Still, have the endurance and patience of Job, my brother. The other side awaits to be revealed to you.

Action Steps

- Reflect on a time when you suffered a tragedy you weren't sure you would bounce back from. Did you recover? If not, ask yourself: "What can I do to begin my healing process today?"
- Read for yourself the Book of Job in the Bible today. You don't have to be a religious man to appreciate this remarkable story.

100. Turn obstacles into opportunities.

The block of granite which is an obstacle in the pathway of the weak becomes a stepping stone in the pathway of the strong.

—Unknown

Life is an obstacle course. It's full of hoops to jump through, stairs to climb, and walls to scale. No matter how much we practice at it, it will always be a challenge. Of that you can be sure. Yet as athletes in the game of life, we have to be vigilant in our quest to finish with flying colors.

The course is filled with stiff competitors in every form imaginable. Classism. Racism. Discrimination. Sexism. Insecurity. Even old "Mr. Jealousy" gains on us along the way.

Keeping ourselves in sharp focus allows us to blur out the competition from running neck-and-neck with us. If we position ourselves straight ahead, we can keep our eyes on the prize no matter how tough the hurdle, how high the wall, or how steep the stair-climb. We can actually draw strength from the gusts of air generated by the competitors around us. Within a single breath we can replenish ourselves with the energy, stamina, and determination we need to turn each obstacle into a golden opportunity.

If you say you want it, why haven't you done it, soldier?

Action Steps

- Stay centered.
- Don't think you can't learn from the competition.
- Play by the rules.
- Give it all ya got!

AFTERWORD

You did then what you knew how to do. When you knew better, you did better.

—Maya Angelou

According to the Centers for Disease Control and Prevention (CDC), there is a disparity in the life expectancies of white men and black men in America. The CDC estimates life expectancy for white men at 73.8 years. Black men live an average of 66.1 years. Think about it. This is nearly an eight-year difference in our respective time spent on earth.

Our own mortality is something to which most of us give very little thought. However, as African Americans, we are frequently reminded of ours. And for good cause. For some reason, because of the color of our skin, black men are prone to having more than our fair share of emotional, physical and spiritual pain and suffering than those of any other racial group. Although the answer of why we seem to be plagued with so many ills is far from simple, we are not destined to live this way.

The new millennium brought with it the opportunity for each of us to start fresh, wipe the slate clean, put the past behind. But like most folks with good intentions, some of our resolutions and goals—if any were made at all—have fallen by the wayside. News flash: African-American men can no longer afford to keep carrying ill emotional, physical and spiritual baggage into the next year, let alone into the next day. It is critical that black men address their issues now. We have to act now, before another generation of us suffers needlessly and dies senselessly as a result of making poor life choices based on ignorance, imbecilic male stubbornness, and pride.

In the grand scheme of things, life is a relatively short journey. In our roles as intelligent men, we get so caught up in trying to be "man enough" and focused on the wrong things in life, that often we live our lives unconsciously. But to echo the words of my brotherfriend Tavis Smiley, each of us was put on this planet for a purpose. I am certain that purpose is to be our best self, and in turn, live our best life. To live your best life means to hold the highest possible vision for yourself. It means that each and every day, each and every hour, each and every minute, each and every *second* you should aspire to greatness in your place in the world. To do so, you must be willing to love, honor and respect yourself enough to make the nurturing of your mind, body and spirit priority number one.

Brothers, if each of us commit to living individual lives, we can reverse the statistics and become role models for young boys as they grow into men—thus ensuring more healthful lives for generations of black men to come. Each of us has a responsibility to ourselves—and to the women and children in our lives who love and care about us—to shape our purpose. It's time we "flip the script" on this planet. Let's remove our Superman capes and direct ourselves toward living the emotionally, physically and spiritually rich lives we were put on earth to enjoy.

With *What Black Men Should Do Now,* you have been given the basic tools to draft your own personal life blueprint, to make much-needed and long-put-off changes. This may be the end of this book, but I hope it marks the beginning of your new, exciting, and empowered life. Go placidly, and with honor.

Take care of yourselves . . . and each other!

K. Thomas Oglesby
May 2002

SUGGESTED READING

The following is a list of books that may shed additional light on the simple truths, ideas, and concepts included in this book:

Akilah, *Journey from Madness to Serenity: A Memoir: Finding Peace in a Manic-Depressive Storm.* Bloomington, IN: 1stBooks Library, 2000.

Alexander, Bill. *A Man's Book of the Spirit: Daily Meditations for a Mindful Life.* New York: Avon, 1994.

Appiah, Kwame Anthony, and Henry Louis Gates Jr. *Africana: The Encyclopedia of the African and African American Experience.* New York: Basic Civitas Books, 1999.

Bates, Karen Grigsby, and Karen E. Hudson. *Basic Black: Home Training for Modern Times.* New York: Broadway Books, 2000.

Bathroom Reader's Institute, The. *Uncle John's Biggest Bathroom Reader,* Berkeley, Cal.: The Bathroom Reader's Institute, 1998.

Bechtel, Stefan; Stains, Laurence, Roy; and the Editors of "Men's Health" books. *Sex: A Man's Guide.* New York: Berkley Books, 1998.

Benton, Walter. *This Is My Beloved.* New York: Random House, 1949.

Bolles, Richard Nelson. *What Color Is Your Parachute? A Practical Manual for Job-Hunters and Career-Changers* (2002 edition). Berkeley, Cal.: Ten Speed Press, 2001.

Boyd, Herb, and Robert L. Allen. *Brotherman: The Odyssey of Black Men in America—An Anthology.* New York: One World, 1996.

Boykin, Keith. *One More River to Cross: Black and Gay in America.* New York: Doubleday, 1998.

Bridges, John. *How to Be a Gentleman.* Nashville, TN: Rutledge Hill Press, 1998.

Brown, Keith Michael. *Sacred Bond: Black Men and Their Mothers.* Boston: Little, Brown, 2000.

Brown, Les. *Live Your Dreams*. New York: Avon Books, 1996.

Bryan, Mark A. *The Prodigal Father: Reuniting Fathers with Their Children*. New York: Three Rivers Press, 1998.

Buursma, Dirk R., and Martha Manikas-Foster. *Men's Devotional Bible: New International Version (NIV)*. Grand Rapids, MI: Zondervan Publishing, 1993.

Carlson, Richard, Ph.D. *Don't Sweat the Small Stuff . . . and It's All Small Stuff*. New York: Hyperion, 1997.

—————. *Don't Sweat the Small Stuff with Your Family: Simple Ways to Keep Daily Responsibilities and Household Chaos from Taking Over Your Life*. New York: Hyperion, 1998.

Childs, Faye, and Noreen Palmer. *Going Off: A Guide for Black Women Who've Just About Had Enough*. New York: St. Martin's Press, 2001.

Cohen, Joseph. *The Penis Book*. Konemann Inc., 1999.

Cole, Harriette. *How To Be: Contemporary Etiquette for African Americans*. New York: Fireside, 2000.

Copage, Eric V. *Black Pearls: Daily Meditations, Affirmations, and Inspirations for African Americans*. New York: Quill, 1993.

—————. *Soul Mates: An Illustrated Guide to Black Love, Sex, and Romance*. New York: Plume, 2001.

Cornish, Dr. Grace. *10 Bad Choices That Ruin Black Women's Lives*. New York: Crown, 1999.

—————. *10 Good Choices That Empower Black Women's Lives*. New York: Crown, 2000.

Covey, Stephen. *The 7 Habits of Highly Effective People: Powerful Lessons in Personal Change*. New York: Fireside, 1990.

Cowie, Colin, and Jean T. Barrett. For the Groom: *A Blueprint for a Gentleman's Lifestyle*. New York: Delacorte Press, 2000.

Daniel, Beverly. *Why Are All The Black Kids Sitting Together in the Cafeteria: And Other Conversations About Race*. Basic Books, 1999.

Daniels, Dawn Marie, and Sandy, Candace. *Souls of My Sisters: Black Women Break Their Silence, Tell Their Stories and Heal Their Spirits*. New York: Kensington, 2000.

Dixon, Barbara M. *Good Health for African Americans*. New York: Crown, 1995.

Dortch, Thomas W., Jr. *The Miracles of Mentoring: How to Encourage and Lead Future Generations*. New York: Broadway Books, 2001.

Dyson, Michael Eric. *Race Rules: Navigating the Color Line.* New York: Addison-Wesley, 1996.

Ellison, Ralph. *Invisible Man.* New York: Vintage Books, 1995.

Elmore, Dr. Ronn. *How to Love a Black Woman: Give—and Get—the Very Best in Your Relationship.* New York: Warner Books, 1999.

Fairley, Juliette. *Money Talks: The Top Black Finance Experts Talk to You about Money.* New York: John Wiley & Sons, 2000.

Fraser, George C. *Race for Success.* New York: Avon Books, 1999.

Gaines, Fabiola Demps, and Roniece Weaver. *The New Soul Food Cookbook for People with Diabetes.* Alexandria, VA: American Diabetes Association, 1999.

Gates, Henry Louis. *Thirteen Ways of Looking at a Black Man.* New York: Vintage Books, 1998.

Givens, Archie. *Spirited Minds: African-American Books for Our Sons and Our Brothers.* New York: Random House, 1998.

Golden, Marita. *Saving Our Sons: Raising Black Children in a Turbulent World.* New York: Anchor Books, 1996.

Graham, Stedman. *You Can Make It Happen: A Nine-Step Plan for Success.* New York: Simon & Schuster, 1998.

Gray, John. *Men Are from Mars, Women Are from Venus: A Practical Guide for Improving Communication and Getting What You Want in Your Relationships.* New York: HarperCollins, 1992.

Green, Bob, and Oprah Winfrey. *Make the Connection: Ten Steps to a Better Body and a Better Life.* New York: Hyperion, 2001.

Harris-Johnson, Debrah. *The African-American Teenagers Guide to Personal Growth, Health, Safety, Sex and Survival: Living and Learning in the 21st Century.* Phoenix, AZ: Amber Books, 2001.

Hayes, Isaac. *Cooking With Heart & Soul.* New York: Putnam Publishing Group, 2000.

Hughes, Dr. Marilyn Hughes, and Porter, Dr. Gayle K. *Prime Time: The African American Woman's Complete Guide To Midlife Health and Wellness.* New York: The Ballantine Publishing Group, 2001.

Hutchinson, Earl Ofari. *The Assassination of the Black Male Image.* New York: Touchstone Books, 1997.

Joannides, Paul. *The Guide to Getting It On!: The Universe's Coolest and Most Informative Book about Sex.* Waldport, OR.: Goofy Foot Press, 2000.

Johnson, Ernest H., Ph.D. *Brothers on the Mend.* New York: Pocket Books, 1998.

Jones, Wilbert. *The Healthy Soul Food Cookbook: How to Cut the Fat but Keep the Flavor.* Secaucus, N.J.: Carol Publishing, 1998.

July, William, II. *Brothers, Lust, and Love: Thoughts on Manhood, Sex, and Romance.* New York: Doubleday, 1998.

———. *Understanding the Tin Man: Why So Many Men Avoid Intimacy.* New York: Broadway Books, 2001.

Kett, Joseph F.; E. D. Hirsch Jr.; and James S. Trefil. *The Dictionary of Cultural Literacy.* Boston: Houghton Mifflin Co., 1993.

Kiyosaki, Robert T., and Sharon L. Lechter. *Rich Dad, Poor Dad: What the Rich Teach Their Kids About Money—That the Poor and Middle Class Do Not!.* New York: Warner Books, 2000.

Kunjufu, Jawanza. *Black Economics: Solutions for Economic and Community Empowerment.* Chicago: African American Images, 1991.

———. *Good Brothers Looking for Good Sisters.* vol. 1, 1997.

Lazear, Jonathon. *Meditations for Men Who Do Too Much.* New York: Fireside, 1992.

Leebow, Ken. *1001 Incredible Things to Do on the Internet.* New York: Warner Books, 2001.

Lockhart, Alexander. *The Portable Pep Talk: Motivational Morsels for Inspiring You to Succeed.* Richmond, Va.: Zander Press, 1997.

Love, Patricia, and Jo Robinson. *Hot Monogamy: Essential Steps to More Passionate, Intimate Lovemaking.* New York: Plume, 1999.

Lyons, Charlotte. *The New Ebony Cookbook.* Chicago: Johnson Publishing Co., 1999.

Madhubuti, Haki R. *Black Men—Obsolete, Single, Dangerous?: The Afrikan American Family in Transition: Essays in Discovery, Solution and Hope.* Chicago Third World Press, 1990.

Maran, Ruth, and Paul Whitehead, and Marangraphics Inc. *Computers Simplified.* Foster City, Cal.: Hungry Minds Inc., 2000.

Marcus, Eric. *Is It a Choice?: Answers to 300 of the Most Frequently Asked Questions About Gay and Lesbian People.* San Francisco: Harper San Francisco, 1999.

McCall, Nathan. *What's Going On: Personal Essays.* New York: Vintage Books, 1999.

McClendon, Joseph, and Anthony Robbins. *Ebony Power Thoughts.* New York: Fireside, 1997.

McGraw, Dr. Phillip C. *Life Strategies: Doing What Works, Doing What Matters.* New York: Hyperion, 2000.

———. *The Life Strategies Workbook: Exercises and Self-Tests to Help You Change Your Life*. New York: Hyperion, 2000.

Milligan, Dr. Rosie. *Satisfying the Black Man Sexually Made Simple*. Los Angeles: Milligan Books, 1994.

———. *Satisfying the Black Woman Sexually Made Simple*. Los Angeles: Milligan Books, 1994.

Millner, Denene, and Nick Chiles. *What Brothers Think, What Sistahs Know About Sex: The Real Deal on Passion, Loving and Intimacy*. New York: Quill, 2000.

Okwu, Julian C. R. *Face Forward: Young African-American Men in a Critical Age*. San Francisco: Chronicle Books, 1997.

Orman, Suze. *The 9 Steps to Financial Freedom: Practical and Spiritual Steps So You Can Stop Worrying*. New York: Three Rivers Press, 2000.

Ozaniec, Naomi, and Deni Bown. *Basic Meditation: 101 Essential Tips*. New York: DK Publishing, 1997.

Phillips, Bill, and Michael D'Orso. *Body For Life: 12 Weeks to Mental and Physical Strength*. New York: HarperCollins, 1999.

Pittman, Frank, M.D. *Man Enough: Fathers, Sons and the Search for Masculinity*. New York: Perigee, 1994.

Pitts, Leonard, Jr. *Becoming Dad: Black Men and the Journey to Fatherhood*. Marietta, GA: Longstreet Press, 1999.

Real, Terrence. *I Don't Want to Talk About It: Overcoming the Secret Legacy of Male Depression*. New York: Fireside, 1998.

Reed, James W., M.D., F.A.C.P.; Neil B. Shulman, M.D.; and Charlene Shucker. *The Black Man's Guide to Good Health: Essential Advice for African-American Men and Their Families*. Roscoe, IL: Hilton Publishing Company, 2000.

Richardson, Cheryl. *Take Time for Your Life: A Personal Coach's Seven-Step Program for Creating the Life You Want*. New York: Broadway Books, 1999.

Rickford, John Russell, and Russell J. Rickford. *Spoken Soul: The Story of Black English*. John Wiley & Sons, Inc., 2000.

Robinson, Randall. *The Debt: What America Owes to Blacks*. New York: Plume, 2001.

Rowan, Dr. Edward L. *The Joy of Self-Pleasuring: Why Feel Guilty About Feeling Good?* Prometheus Books, 2000.

Ruiz, Miguel, and Don Miguel Ruiz. *The Four Agreements—A Practical Guide to Personal Freedom: A Toltec Wisdom Book*. New York: Amber-Allen Publishing Inc., 1997.

Schlenger, Sunny, and Roberta Roesch. *How to Be Organized in Spite of Yourself: Time and Space Management That Works with Your Personal Style.* New York: Signet, 1999.

Schwartz, David, Ph.D. *The Magic of Thinking Big.* New York: Fireside, 1987.

Schwartz, Dr. Pepper, and Dominic Cappello. *Ten Talks Parents Must Have with Their Children About Sex and Character.* New York: Hyperion, 2000.

Sheehy, Gail. *Understanding Men's Passages: Discovering the New Map of Men's Lives.* New York: Ballantine Books, 1999.

Shinn, Florence Scovel. *The Game of Life and How to Play It.* Beekman Publishing, Inc., 1999.

Smiley, Tavis. *How to Make Black America Better: Leading African Americans Speak Out.* New York: Doubleday, 2001.

Smith, Dr. George Edmond. *Walking Proud: Black Men Living Beyond the Stereotypes.* New York: Kensington, 2001.

Spizman, Robyn Freedan. *The Perfect Present: The Ultimate Gift Guide For Every Occasion.* New York: Crown, 1998.

Spohn, David. *Touchstones: A Book of Daily Meditations for Men.* Center City, MN: Hazelden Publishing, 1996.

St. James, Elaine. *Living the Simple Life: A Guide to Scaling Down and Enjoying More.* New York: Hyperion, 1998.

Toropov, Brandon, and Father Luke. *The Complete Idiot's Guide to World Religions.* New York: Macmillan Publishing USA, 2001.

Tyndale House Publishers. *Life Application Study Bible: New International Version (NIV).* Carol Stream, Illinois: Tyndale House Publishers, 1997.

Vanzant, Iyanla. *Acts of Faith: Daily Meditations for People of Color.* New York: Fireside, 1993.

————. *The Spirit of a Man: A Vision of Transformation for Black Men and the Women Who Love Them.* San Francisco: HarperCollins, 1997.

Walsh, Dr. Patrick C. *Dr. Patrick Walsh's Guide to Surviving Prostate Cancer.* New York: Warner Books, 2001.

West, Cornel. *Race Matters.* New York: Vintage Books, 1994.

Wilkinson, Bruce. *The Prayer of Jabez: Breaking Through to the Blessed Life.* Sisters, OR: Multnomah Publishers, Inc., 2000.

Williams, Angel Kyodo. *Being Black: Zen and the Art of Living With Fearlessness and Grace.* New York: Viking Press, 2000.

Williams, Montel, and Wini Linguvic. *BodyChange: The 21-day Program for Changing Your Body and Changing Your Life!* Carlsbad, CA: Mountain Movers Press, 2001.

Zahler, Diane, and Zahler, Kathy. *Test Your Cultural Literacy.* (2nd Edition). New York: Arco, 1993.

Zukav, Gary. *The Seat of the Soul.* New York: Fireside, 1990.

REFERRALS

Here's a list of telephone numbers that you may find helpful:

American Cancer Society, 800-ACS-2345
American Heart Association, 800-242-8721
American Coalition for Fathers & Children, 800-978-DADS (3237)
American Diabetes Association, 800-DIABETES (342-2383)
Black Mental Health Alliance for Education and Consultation
    Inc., 410-837-2642
Centers for Disease Control and Prevention National STD and
    AIDS Hotline, 800-342-AIDS (2437)
Child Help USA National Child Abuse Hotline, 800-422-4453
Consumer Credit Counseling Services, 800-284-1723
End Abuse Helpline, 800-END-ABUSE
National Cancer Institute, 800-4-CANCER
National Clearinghouse for Alcohol and Drug Information, 800-
    729-6686
National Council on Alcohol and Drug Dependence, 800-729-6686
National Council on Sexual Addiction and Compulsivity, 770-989-
    9754
National Domestic Violence Hotline, 800-799-SAFE (7233); TTY
    for the hearing-impaired: 800-787-3224
National Mental Health Information Line, 800-421-4211
National Mentoring Partnership, 877-BE-A-MENT (232-6368)
National Organization for Victim Assistance, 800-TRY-NOVA
    (879-6682)
National Suicide Prevention Hotline, 800-SUICIDE (784-2433)
Planned Parenthood, 800-230-PLAN (7526)
Prostate Health Council/American Foundation for Urologic Dis-
    ease, 800-242-2383

INDEX OF QUOTES

1. Copage, Eric. *Black Pearls: Daily Meditations, Affirmations, and Inspirations for African Americans.* New York: Quill, 1993.
2. *Direct Wire.* Atlanta: August/September, 1998.
3. Robbins, Anthony, and Joseph McClendon III. *Ebony Power Thoughts.* New York: Fireside, 1997.
4. Bell, Janet Cheatham. *Famous Black Quotations.* New York: Warner Books, 1995.
5. *USA Today.* Arlington, Va.: September 2, 1998.
6. Copage, Eric. *Black Pearls.*
7. Terry, Rod. *Brother's Keeper: Words of Inspiration for African-American Men.* White Plains, N.Y.: Peter Pauper Press, 1996.
8. *In Style.* New York: November, 1998.
9. Eli, Quinn. *Many Strong and Beautiful Voices.* Philadelphia: Running Press, 1997.
10. *Ebony.* Chicago: July, 1997.
11. Terry, Rod. *Brother's Keeper.*
12. Braude, Jacob M. *Complete Speaker's and Toastmaster's Library.* Englewood Cliffs, N.J.: Prentice-Hall, 1977.
13. *Today's Black Woman.* Paramus, N.J.: September, 1996.
14. *Book of Familiar Quotations.* New York: Award Books, 1970.
15. Cole, Johnnetta B. *Dream The Boldest Dreams and Other Lessons of Life.* Atlanta: Longstreet Press, 1997.
16. Braude, Jacob M. *Complete Speaker's and Toastmaster's Library.*
17. Source unknown.
18. Robbins, Anthony, and Joseph McClendon III. *Ebony Power Thoughts.*
19. Copage, Eric. *Black Pearls Journal.* New York: William Morrow, 1995.

20. *Ebony.* Chicago: May, 1997.
21. Robbins, Anthony, and Joseph McClendon III. *Ebony Power Thoughts.*
22. Copage, Eric. *Black Pearls Journal.*
23. Source unknown.
24. Braude, Jacob M. *Complete Speaker's and Toastmaster's Library.*
25. *Vibe* magazine online: www.vibe.com. New York: December, 1994.
26. Copage, Eric. *Black Pearls.*
27. Kimbro, Dennis. *Daily Motivations for African-American Success.* New York: Fawcett Crest, 1993.
28. Copage, Eric. *Black Pearls.*
29. Elmore, Dr. Ronn. *How to Love a Black Man.* New York: Warner Books, 1997.
30. Eli, Quinn. *Many Strong and Beautiful Voices.*
31. Ibid.
32. Ibid.
33. Jordan, Michael. *I Can't Accept Not Trying.* New York: Random House, 1996.
34. Kimbro, Dennis. *Daily Motivations for African-American Success.*
35. *Essence.* New York: November, 1998.
36. Braude, Jacob M. *Complete Speaker's and Toastmaster's Library.*
37. Ibid.
38. Terry, Rod. *Brother's Keeper.*
39. Ibid.
40. Source unknown.
41. *The Flip Wilson Show*
42. Source unknown.
43. Source unknown.
44. *The Oprah Winfrey Show*
45. Kimbro, Dennis. *Daily Motivations for African-American Success.*
46. Source unknown.
47. Robbins, Anthony, and Joseph McClendon III. *Ebony Power Thoughts.*
48. Philippians 3:13.
49. *Ebony.* Chicago: July, 1997.
50. Source unknown.
51. Copage, Eric. *Black Pearls Journal.*
52. Terry, Rod. *Brother's Keeper.*

53. Source unknown.
54. Terry, Rod. *Brother's Keeper.*
55. Braude, Jacob M. *Complete Speaker's and Toastmaster's Library.*
56. Lowe, Janet. *Oprah Winfrey Speaks.* New York: John Wiley & Sons, 1998.
57. Braude, Jacob M. *Complete Speaker's and Toastmaster's Library.*
58. Vanzant, Iyanla. *The Spirit Of A Man.*
59. Source unknown.
60. Copage, Eric. *Black Pearls.*
61. Ibid.
62. Cottman, Michael H. *Million Man March.* New York: Crown, 1995.
63. Source unknown.
64. Isley Brothers. *Isley Brothers 60's: Greatest Hits And Rare Classics.* Detroit: Motown Records, 1991.
65. *Ebony.* Chicago: August, 1991.
66. Kimbro, Dennis. *Daily Motivations for African-American Success.*
67. Avery, Byllye. *An Altar of Words.* New York: Broadway, 1998.
68. Cole, Johnnetta B. *Dream The Boldest Dreams.*
69. Terry, Rod. *Brother's Keeper.*
70. Copage, Eric. *Black Pearls Journal.*
71. Copage, Eric. *Black Pearls.*
72. McWilliams, Peter. *The Life 101 Quote Book.* Los Angeles: Prelude Press, 1996.
73. Copage, Eric. *Black Pearls Journal.*
74. Source unknown.
75. Terry, Rod. *Brother's Keeper.*
76. Avery, Byllye. *An Altar of Words.*
77. Copage, Eric. *Black Pearls.*
78. Cole, Johnnetta B. *Dream The Boldest Dreams.*
79. *Essence.* New York: November, 1998.
80. Delany, Sarah, A. Elizabeth Delany, and Amy Hill Hearth. *The Delany Sisters' Book of Everyday Wisdom.* New York: Kodansha International, 1994.
81. *Jet.* Chicago: April 28, 1997.
82. U.S. Census Bureau.
83. Source unknown.
84. Source unknown.
85. Copage, Eric. *Black Pearls.*

86. Source unknown.
87. Copage, Eric. *Black Pearls Journal.*
88. Office of the U.S. Surgeon General.
89. Delany, Sarah, A. Elizabeth Delany, and Amy Hill Hearth. *The Delany Sisters' Book of Everyday Wisdom.*
90. Eddie Robinson Web site: www.eddierobinson.org/quotes. html.
91. Copage, Eric. *Black Pearls.*
92. *Essence.* New York: November, 1998.
93. Leslau, Charlotte, and Wolf Leslau. *African Proverbs.* White Plains, N.Y.: Peter Pauper Press, Inc., 1985.
94. Bell, Janet Cheatham. *Famous Black Quotations.*
95. Terry, Rod. *Brother's Keeper.*
96. Kimbro, Dennis. *Daily Motivations for African-American Success.*
97. Braude, Jacob M. *Complete Speaker's and Toastmaster's Library.*
98. Source unknown.
99. Source unknown.
100. Source unknown.

Index

7908305R0

Made in the USA
Lexington, KY
21 December 2010